OBAMA IS A BIG STUPID POOPY PANTS
(I WROTE THIS BOOK IN 3 DAYS)

by

Mike Lawrence

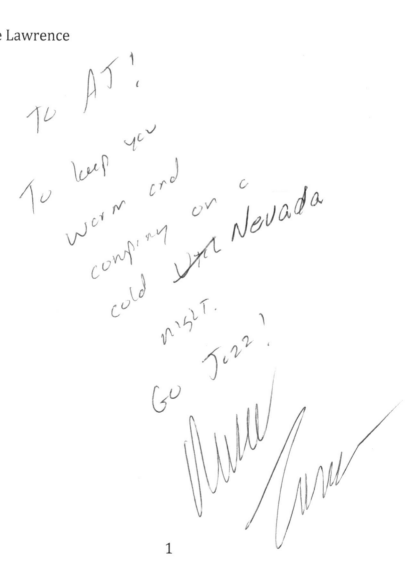

TABLE OF CONTENTS

Introduction

Chapter 1
Obama, he's stupid

Chapter 2
Spouses are off limits. That's why I won't say Michelle Obama is ugly.

Chapter 3
Facts. The REAL F-word

Chapter 4
Fox News: What a buncha liberals.

Chapter 5
CNN: Extremists

Chapter 6
MSNBC: Rachel Maddow's gay. Need I say more?

Chapter 7:
My solution: the All-Speculation News Network

Chapter 8
Jon Stewart: He just pisses me off

Chapter 9
Where the hell is the flag lapel pin?

Chapter 10
Obama plays the blame game, and that's a reason why everything is his fault.

Chapter 11
Janet Jackson's Boob = Teen Pregnancy

The world will implode if we let two dudes get married.

Chapter 59
Tax cuts cured my impotence.

Chapter 60
Obamacare = death to all

Chapter 61
Support the Troops. By sending them to war.

Chapter 62
Cheney, Dick

Chapter 63
Evolution is just a theory, like gravity

Chapter 64
The Dixie Chicks: Three mean-spirited bitches.

Chapter 65
"Happy Holidays" = WAR!

Chapter 66
The solution? ME!

Introduction

Every night I go to bed thankful I'm still alive.

Because every day under an Obama presidency, there's a 50/50 chance that the world will erupt into a giant fireball, turning us all into a one giant cinder pile. This is the constant fear I live with. And I am not alone. And that is why I wrote this book.

People have many opinions on Barack Obama. They range from those who say he's a bad president to those who say he's the worst president ever. Going beyond the political, many say he's a bad person. And there are those who say he's the worst person alive today. Those people are entitled to their opinions.

But I did not spend three days of my life writing this book for them. I wrote this for those who believe Obama is the worst person in history of the world, and will be the worst person there ever was. Because only people like me know this truth, and have the guts to say it. Sure, calling Obama the worst person alive is a nice start, but it tells me you lack passion behind your convictions.

Some may call my views extreme. But I'm really not. I'm quite normal, as I keep having to tell people. But guess what? Other people have views even more "radical" than me. For example, they're the ones who think Obama is not just the worst person, but the worst *living thing* of all time. That's silly. The worst living thing ever was JAWS. Or Lord Voldemort. Obama isn't quite in their league.

However, what we can all agree on is that Obama is destroying America. That's not even debatable. But the big question is how. How is he taking this once great nation and turning it into a trash heap?

I believe it's because he is a big stupid poopy pants.

He's no genius. He's not the smartest guy in the room, unless that room is empty. Or full of tree-hugging, flag-burning, no-child-labor-loving liberals. HA! (I say HA because I'm not really sure how to make that smiley-face thingy with my keyboard. So whenever I say HA, it means I made sort of a joke.)

So Obama's stupidity, backed by his poopy-pants nature, is destroying America. It's not some grand plan. He's just stupid. Not Forest Gump stupid. Just stupid in the way all liberals are stupid, in that they don't see the Truth, the Truth that's been covered up beneath the layers of so-called history, reporting, common knowledge, common sense and facts. It's a privilege to know this Truth, and we then have a responsibility to share it with others, and save America from stupid poopy pants Obama.

This book delivers a point of view that until now never had a true voice. I've seen what people like Ann Coulter, Glenn Beck, Michael Savage and Rush Limbaugh are doing and saying and writing and accusing. And it's a good start. But they're a bunch of pansies! (I respect them all, however, and would love to promote my book on their radio shows, if I could just get past their screeners). They hold back their criticism, always soft-pedaling and never saying what they really mean. Calling Obama a racist? *Is that all you got?* Calling him Halfrican? Calling him terrorist, socialist, born in Kenya? We could be doing so much better by calling Obama so much worse.

And that's what this book does. It says what those people won't say, or are too afraid to say. And this book offers solutions that our great minds haven't even considered. Maybe after what I've written hits the world, Limbaugh and Coulter and Savage and Beck and Bozell and O'Reilly and Hannity and Ingraham and that other blond woman... Monica Something... you know the one that sounds like she's faking a deep voice but it's really how her voice sounds, and Palin and Huckabee and all the rest of them can break free of the verbal shackles that bind them and say what they really mean, what most of America needs to know. That Obama is a big stupid poopy pants.

Like the title said, I wrote this book in three days. You may wonder how. Well for starters, I didn't do any of that RESEARCH like those Ivy League eggheads from UCLA would do. Nope, I shoot from the hip. My facts come from what I know, not from what I had to find out. Plus research takes a lot of time. It's stupid. Research is not the boss of me.

This book proves that Obama is stupid, and just for good measure, also shows how our out-of-touch lamestream* media let a stupid poopy pants like him in the White House. Plus there's a lot of other stuff. And I tried to keep the chapters short. But at times I tend to ramble, which is fine with me. That's just more wasted paper to really piss off those stupid tree-huggers. HA!

*The word "Lamestream" courtesy of she who breathes light and goodness, Ms. Sarah Palin.

CHAPTER 1
Obama, he's stupid

"They" say Obama went to Harvard. Like that means he's smart. If that's the truth, name me some smart people who graduated from Harvard.

I'm waiting.

See, it's not that easy.

And get this... he hasn't released his "college transcripts", which is a fancy way to say "grades." You know what kind of a person keeps his grades a secret? A stupid person. When I was a kid, if I had a bad report card, I would hide it from my parents. If I got good grades, I'd show it to them. "Look Ma, a B in gym."

So if he got good grades, he would show them to us. But he didn't, so he won't. So that proves he's stupid. I rest my case, your honor.

And if he were so smart, why would he work as a social worker in Chicago, organizing communities? There's no money in that! He could have worked a real job making a ton of money with his Harvard education, but didn't. Given the choice between two jobs where one of them pays more, which would *you* choose? Yeah, me too. But then again, you and I aren't stupid.

And what does it mean to "organize communities"? I'm not sure how you organize a community. ("OK, you people will live here. A bookstore will go here. And a dilapidated, rust-filled playground will go here.") It sounds fishy to me. Like some mumbo jumbo made-up job title, like assistant to the vice president, or elementary school teacher.

And liberal rags like the Wall Street Journal contend that Obama was president of the Harvard Law Review. Big deal (even if it's true)! That doesn't sound so hard! I can review laws too. A law against kidnapping? That's a good law. Thumbs up from me. Same with laws against murder. And smoking pot.

I like those laws. See, anyone can review a law. Just call me Judge Lawrence.

Meanwhile, a lot of people say Obama "leads from behind." I'm not sure what that means, but it does make him sound stupid. Doesn't he know you're not leading when you're not in front? You're just pushing things.

Either way, Obama shows how stupid he is when he opens his mouth. Did you know he thinks the US has 57 states? He said so! It's on tape. It must have been one of those times he didn't have his *teleprompter* with him. HA! That's right. I went there.

See, because Obama doesn't go the extra mile to memorize a 30-minute speech, he's forced to use a teleprompter. Just like Ron "Stay classy, San Diego" Burgundy. So at least Obama knows how to read. He's stupid but literate!

Now I understand that other presidents have used teleprompters (Clinton, Carter), but as a conservative, it's just too much fun bringing it up in a crowd of liberals. If a liberal has some momentum going on an argument, just say, "Did you read that off a teleprompter, like Obama would?" That just gets the liberal mad. And then he can't resist going off on a tangent as he tries to put you in your place about the whole teleprompter crack. The "Obama uses a teleprompter" is our new "Al Gore invented the Internet". Hell, I know the true story (Al Gore invented nothing... he was just a congressman who pushed for Internet development, and the whole invention thing was taken out of context), but I just love hearing a liberal get all huffy and explain it to me again. It's cute to see them all riled up.

But the teleprompter is serious business. It doesn't just reflect on Obama's intellect. It reveals his work ethic as well. It means he's lazy. Lazy and stupid. Add drunk to the mix and Obama is more like Bluto Blutarsky that Alfred Einstein.

And I for one do not want a stupid and lazy president. That's why I DEMAND a president who will never ever use a teleprompter. And he must be a Republican. I think we'd all like to see that happen.

CHAPTER 2
Spouses are off limits.
That's why I won't say Michelle Obama is ugly.

As we've proven already, Barack Obama is a stupid poopy pants. But what can you call somebody who *marries* him? Mrs. Stupid Poopy Pants? No. We call her Michelle Obama.

This chapter is hard for me to write. Because this is a book about Barack Obama. So spouses and children and pets should be off limits. It's not morally right to say anything bad about them.

Unless...

It's the truth.

Then you HAVE TO say something! It's your duty. Like telling someone her new hairdo is an argument for baldness.

As we all know, Michelle Obama has made herself to be a "hands-on" First Lady, sticking her nose where it don't belong. To this end, she has taken up a cause that truly is a dastardly evil plan, one that's so heinous it makes us genuine Americans shiver in fear as we cradle our trembling children to protect them from an onslaught worse than a trillion simultaneous nuclear holocausts: She wants us to cut down on desserts.

I'll give you a minute to let the horror of that sink in.

Who the hell does she think she is? Our Mom? Well if she's our Mom, then I'm her smartass kid telling her to "Shove it, I never asked to be born in this family!" I don't even care if I get grounded.

What's next, telling us not to smoke a cigarette after dinner? Telling us it'll fall off if we keep playing with it? Telling us to learn to read, go to rehab or just say no to drugs? That's crazy talk, especially coming from a First Lady.

Now I've heard the braying and prattling on from the left. They claim we're twisting Michelle Obama's words. That she's not dictating what we should eat (You know who else dictated? Hitler!). Instead they say she's just advising us that as

13

more adults and children in our country get fatter, and obesity rates climb, and diabetes rates go up with them to create spiraling health care costs, we should be aware of what we're putting in our bodies, and should moderate how much sugar, fat and Bloomin' Onions we consume. And to those people I say, "Shut up."

In fact, I think Michelle is CAUSING us to get fatter. Because the more she talks about fatty, greasy, yummy foods, and tasty sweet candy, the more tempted I get to eat a big plate of it. And then I want to double down on cheese fries and double up on desserts. See, it's suggestive selling! Like when the waitress asks if you'd like another beer, but you were planning to leave pretty soon, but because *she* put the thought in your head (foul temptress!), you have one more. A tall one. One that's ice cold and delicious and so worth it and I'm now so relaxed and confident and I think it's time I quit my job and where'd I put my keys and hey maybe that waitress thinks I'm cute I should ask her out and I think I'm going to be sick oh will SOMEONE PLEASE STOP SPINNING THE ROOM!

So Michelle Obama, in her diabolical way, is making things worse by claiming to make things better. I think she actually wants us to get fatter, so then she can brag even more about how awesome her arms look.

Which is why I think some news organizations should do the nation a great service by letting us know any time Michelle Obama has a cheeseburger, or dessert, or a bowl of Frosted Flakes. In fact, I think we need a 24-hour news channel that is only dedicated to her nutritional hypocrisy. If she wants to hold us to a higher standard, we need to do the same to her. With hidden cameras and videotape. It's the American way!

That same channel could also cover the way she travels all over the world, jet-setting like she's some dignitary or head of state. She's just a wife! Of a head of state. When other world leaders visit the U.S., do they bring their wives? I don't think so!

And do you see what it costs for Michelle to travel? It's not like you or me (which is expensive enough, even if we fly Southwest where bags fly free... I'm holding you to that, Southwest! Once you charge for bags, it's over between us!).

Michelle packs like some sort of princess, with casual wear for the day AND a different dress for every night of the week. And because people hate her enough to kill her, she needs Secret Service detail! So *that's* expensive. And if she takes her daughters Sasha and the other one, those two need Secret Service, too. It's ridiculous. Those trips cost thousands of dollars, coming off the taxpayer's dime. Hope you had a good time, girls! Take pictures and post them to your Facebook account, so we can see the trip you took. That we paid for! Maybe Michelle should quit all the gallivanting around and spend more time busting her ass First Ladying.

Because the First Lady's place is in the home. Her White Home. She shouldn't be going anywhere. Just stay in the White House, wait for Barack to get home, and offer him a beer and a Kenyan foot massage. And clean the place up a bit. Why hire all those expensive (taxpayer-funded) housekeepers when Michelle can do a little dusting?

CHAPTER 3
Facts... the REAL F-word

Nothing bothers me more than when I make a point, and some smartass comes right back with a "fact" that makes me look dumb. Here's an example:

I was with some people at Cici's (is it me, or have the "Welcome to Cici's" been a little less exuberant lately?), and I made the point that invading Iraq was the right thing to do because Saddam Hussein helped knock down the Twin Towers.

Immediately some smartypants at the table next to me says, "Um, I couldn't help but overhear what you said. Saddam had nothing to do with 9/11. In fact, he and bin Laden were practically enemies. It was all in the 9/11 Commission's Report. Just thought you should know."

If I'm being honest, that was embarrassing, especially in front of my buddies. And it really got under my skin, even after we dragged him to the Cici's arcade and kicked the shit out of him. Where the hell does he get off telling me I'm wrong in front of my friends, and then having the gall to pretend there is some important-sounding source to back him up?

That's why, when I get in a political argument, I try to keep my facts to a minimum. Because no one likes a know-it-all. Remember the smartest kid in your class, the one who reminded the teacher there was a test today? No one liked him. Recess Justice took care of that clown.

Besides, the purpose of an argument is to show how passionate you are about a topic. It's not about being "right." And where does passion come from? It comes from the heart. And from yelling. Lots of yelling, and interruptions, and sarcastic head-shaking and exaggerated eye-rolling and vigorous finger-pointing. That's how you win.

Truth be told, it's hard to get passionate about facts. They're boring. And so full of precise numbers. And you have to "source" them. Face it, I don't have time to give you a book report. I have ten seconds to make my point, shut you up, and

16

get the hell out of there. That's what makes for good political discourse in this country. Facts? Facts are for bookworms, and science journals no one reads.

And Obama comes across as the most bookwormish of all. Even after all this time, this guy *still* seems to believe we care about facts. He throws numbers around, shows us charts, and delivers "facts" right off the top of his head so smoothly, you just know he's making shit up. Because no one could know all that! It's impossible. And because of this, Obama has shown his hand.

You see, if he wasn't too much of a stupid poopy pants he would realize that spouting off facts as if he actually knew them doesn't fly around here. Since it's impossible for one person to know so much, the only rational explanation is that he's LYING. He's just pulling stuff out of his ass. So we know we can't believe him when he says one in every five American kids live below the poverty level (there he goes, using numbers again), or when he says the war in Afghanistan has been fought for over 10 years, or when he says his birthday is August 4. In fact (no pun intended, HA!), I have a simple rule on what to believe when Obama speaks: nothing. Since he lies 99% of the time, that just means I'm wrong about what to believe 1% of the time.

So now that we're done talking about facts, let's talk about Fox News.

CHAPTER 4
Fox News.
What a buncha liberals.

The emergence of Fox New is truly the great American success story. It began in 1996. And thanks to one very special blowjob, it became the most watched news network in history.

But that success may have also corrupted it. Because once it started to be taken as a serious news organization, it was obligated to try and act like one. You know, by being objective. By showing us both sides of the story. By sourcing its information. All the rules that take the fun out of news.

Now some say that Fox News is just a right-wing propaganda machine. I wish! On their best day, Fox News is a moderate voice of reason, but on most days, it's liberal tripe.

Fair and Balanced? Maybe if your idea of "fair" is giving equal time to those who say Obama is a Muslim terrorist, and to those who feel he's merely an un-American Socialist. In some circles, this might be showing "both sides of the story." But what about giving airtime to those who say Obama has committed genocide, or is gay?

So while Fox News leans left, it's still the news channel I watch the most. Next in my viewing order is Fox Business Channel, followed by Fox Sports. But not the Spice Channel. I don't know how that got on there.

But despite their liberal bias, I can find some shred of journalistic integrity in just about all their shows throughout the day.

Fox & Friends

The day starts with Fox & Friends. It's a nice premise, where Gretchen Carlson has two charismatic men (Steve and Brian) teaching her the finer points of politics and current events in simple terms that even she can understand. They even let her ask some questions to the guests, to make her feel included, which has to help her self-esteem. That's why they're her "Friends." But while Gretchen is pretty, I wouldn't call her a "Fox." So I'm not sure the title is totally accurate.

Steve Doocey is the smart one, the senior leader of the show -- think Freddy driving the Mystery Machine –– who puts things into layman's terms. Steve's a perfect-looking specimen, almost like a robot sent from the future to make America a better place. He's a teacher of sorts, without the union giving him a free ride for showing up. Co-host Brian Kilmeade is like the rambunctious teaching assistant, who's always got Steve's back, and dumbs down what Steve is saying even more for members of the audience, and Gretchen too. "So to clarify, if USC scores more points against UCLA, that means they win."

But personality-wise, the whole crew is just too nice. Never once have they called for the assassination of Obama. NOT ONCE. Not even to put it out there, or even subtly slide it in as a question/tease before they go to commercial. Seriously, couldn't Brian just say, "We'll whip up a batch of holiday sugar cookies, and discuss the best way to assassinate Obama, after the break." See, no one gets hurt there!

Regardless, Fox & Friends is the fastest, snarkiest 180 minutes on television. And it's a decent source for veiled, passive-aggressive assaults on liberals.

American Newsroom
After Fox & Friends, it's time to get serious. DEADLY SERIOUS. And that's what we get with the more news-stories-of-the-day-oriented American Newsroom.

That's right, bitches. "AMERICAN Newsroom." Not some Al GoreJazeera station. If you're a true patriot, you'll get your news from a real American Newsroom. Not some newsroom in China, or Mexico, or Atlanta. USA! USA! Ted Nugent!

American Newsroom is able to take all the gossipy, conversational, unsubstantiated parts of "Fox & Friends" and make it sound like real news. In fact, they take the baton from F&F and keep it going for the next leg. Like if Steve Doocey asks, "Do people think Obama is an asshole?", it sparks a passionate conversation on Fox & Friends, where people debate if Obama is a major asshole, or a totally major asshole. So by the time "American Newsroom" rolls around, they're able to give us the first of forty FOX NEWS ALERTS of the day, dropping a hint as to what America is now talking about: "Americans think Obama is an asshole." Technically this is factually accurate. There are people who think Obama is an asshole. And they are technically Americans. So nothing inaccurate with the ALERT syntax. Sure, the headline may IMPLY that ALL Americans think Obama is an asshole. But that's just semantics. It's open to interpretation. Which is why Fox lets their viewers decide what the facts are.

Best of all, because that "Obama is an asshole" alert is on a *real* news show, that makes it genuine news, and therefore true. Obama *is* an asshole. A major one at the least. That's dynamite reporting right there. For being a liberal news network, Fox News has some good ideas.

One aside here. Fox News Alerts are only for the most important, earth-shattering news-breaking events of the day. It's not something to be used willy-nilly to manipulate the public into judging one news item more important than the other. Plus a Fox News viewer's time is incredibly important, so a Fox News Alert can't be wasted on trivial matters MICHAEL LOHAN GAVE CRACK TO LINDSEY?!

That's why a Fox News Alert only appears on stories that affect the whole world in significant and possibly grave ways RED LOBSTER HAS ALL YOU CAN EAT SHRIMP AGAIN?! And when it's a Fox News Alert, you know it's important. Because it interrupts the current newscast (if not the commercials). Bill Hemmer could be interviewing the Pope, who's admitting to personally sodomizing altar boys in the Vatican Foosball Room, and even that isn't enough to prevent a Fox News Alert from letting us know LEFT-HANDED PEOPLE HAVE MORE SATISFYING SEX LIVES. Because news like that can never wait.

American Newsroom is hosted by Bill Hemmer. He's a good-looking guy, with cheekbones that appear chiseled from the stonecutting tools of Michelangelo and skin as smooth as fine leather oiled to a delicious shine (I'm not gay). It's like Clark Kent broke free of the newspaper business and went into television. Which is a smart move on his part, because from what I hear, newspapers are dying. Makes sense, with all that reading involved. Get to the point, newspapers! Stop with all the words. If you can't tell me everything in 30 seconds, it couldn't have been that important. Also, it's your fault if I don't understand what the article is about. You should have explained it better.

Martha MacCallum helps Bill out on the show, playing the part of "Girl Newscaster". While I'd like her to look a little more like Lois Lane, to complete my clever Superman analogy, she does a decent job looking pretty. Which one can never overstate. Fact: If the person delivering the news isn't nice enough to look at (at least if she's a girl), then people won't listen. It's like a tree falling in the forest with no one around to hear it. If Christiane Amanpour says something insightful and amazing, who cares?

Happening Now
At first I thought this was a rerun of American Newsroom, but if you look closely, they have different anchors. But the news stories are the same, with an occasional update and about seven Fox News Alerts IS YOUR BATHROOM GIVING YOU CANCER? NO. "Happening Now" is the perfect news show in case you've slept in.

Co-host Jon Scott is a fairly talented guy with experience. I know he has experience because I can swear I've seen him somewhere else before. I'm just not sure where or when. Plus he has a great news anchor name. It's quick, to the point, and doesn't waste too many letters (No H in "Jon", though he could take one of the T's off "Scott").

Jenna Lee is the co-anchor and is real cute. She may be one of the 10 prettiest women on Fox News. Here's proof she's pretty: I can never remember a single thing she says.

And having a name like Jenna means one of two things: you're either in porn, or you're on Fox News.

America Live
Until Obama became president, this was called America Live, where the "Live" is said with a long "I" sound. Now that Obama is killing this country, I call it America Live (with the short I sound), as in "America, don't you die on me, LIVE!"

This is also known as the time of day I like to call "Unplug the Phone and Tune Into Megyn Kelly". She is a goddess, created by God on the Seventh Day and kept on a shelf in Heaven until the time was right to bring her unto the world. In the form of an anchor with her own news-reading show in the afternoon on a cable news channel.

What does the Y in Megyn stands for? It stands for "Y don't you ever answer my letters?" Seriously, how often do I have to re-tweet her tweets or Photoshop her on my blog before she acknowledges that I exist?

She's the best. And it's not just because she's pretty. It's also because she has nice legs. And you can see them through that plexiglass desk of hers. Greta Van Susteren doesn't have one of those desks.

Megyn does it all. Delivers the news. Interviews people. Slyly includes a bit of commentary in such a way that only the most perceptive (yours truly) can get it. Like after she delivers the news on Michelle Obama's latest European junket to Awesomeland, Megyn will glance away at the papers in front of her, remove the smile from her face, and say, "Good use of tax dollars, if you know what I mean?" Yeah, I know what you mean, MK.

"America Live" proves that a woman doesn't need a man. Megyn has no male co-host (though 99% of people she interviews are men). However, I saw her once ask a tough question of a Republican, and the guy squirmed a bit, but luckily a commercial break or Fox News Alert GOLD IS AWESOME BUY SOME BUY SOME BUY SOME ended the segment just in time. Phew, that was close. But Megyn is human... we all make a mistake sometimes. I forgive her.

Studio B with Shepard Smith.
Shep is awful. They need to "shepherd" him on out of there (HA!). He's got that smarmy, nasally I'm-so-smart voice, which he uses to deliver the radical view on just about everything. Like he may ask a guest about ending tax cuts! ENDING TAX CUTS! Like it's even an option. He might as well ask the guest to eat his own children. He'll even "push back" on Republican guests (not just the Democrats), going so far as to ask follow-up questions, as if their answers weren't enough. The gall of this guy. Maybe that's why he's in Studio B, and not Studio A. Because Studio B stands for "bullshit."

I don't like Shep's haircut, either. Just thought you should know. Makes him look like some lab-generated man-child.

Your World with Neil Cavuto

Neil Cavuto is really smart. You can tell because he wears glasses. He knows a lot about money and can always bring the day's news back to finances. Like if Paris Hilton breaks her parole or if it's spring break time, Neil can spend 5 minutes relating it back to the day's Market Watch. Genius. Plus he always has accompanying footage to go with it. I tell you, a segment on derivatives is a lot more enjoyable when a few bikini babes are jiggling their behinds on the splitscreen.

Neil must be a billionaire, because he knows so much about the economy and how markets work. If he's following his own advice on investing, he must be loaded. I'm sure that his gig on Fox is some sort of side job or hobby. He doesn't need the money; he's just bored, or feels he's doing a public service. And for that, we all owe him our thanks. And a broker's fee.

The Five (Formerly Glenn Beck)

I wore a black armband the day Glenn Beck was taken off the air at Fox. And I did cry a little. He and I didn't always see eye-to-eye (He once said "I think Obama is a racist"; however, I *know* it to be true), but I like that he treated his audience like adults, using a chalkboard to explain things.

Those chalkboard discussions really opened my eyes to how dangerous this world is, and how we're on the precipice of disaster... always on the precipice, never quite going over, but always so *close*. Anyway, with the Chalkboard Wisdom, we learned that Obama is just a few Kevin Bacon-game connections removed from Hitler. I didn't know this, and would have thought it to be preposterous, until Beck pointed it out. See, Obama once wore a red tie, which we all know is the color of Communism. Communism is Russian. And Obama is always rushin' to get somewhere. And Joseph Stalin was Russian, who massacred 20 million people. He was bad. And Hitler was bad too, massacring 6 million people. So, ergo, Obama is like Hitler and Stalin put together, and is responsible for the massacre of 26 million people (so far). See, the logic is ironclad. It's on The Chalkboard.

Anyway, the days of Beck on Fox News are gone. I guess what he was dishing out was just too radioactive for too many people. The truth often is. Now Beck's timeslot is taken up by a show called The Five. This is a very clever title, because it comes on at 5pm, AND it has five people, in a sort of roundtable discussion that proves it takes at least five mortals to replace one Glenn Beck.

However, this show has liberal leanings, which doesn't always make for a fair fight in my eyes. Of the five, four are "conservatives" and one is a "liberal." While some may see this as "fair and balanced" I don't see it that way. Fair and balanced should represent the makeup of America, and based on what I know about this country (based mostly from watching Fox News and surfing various web sites and emails from friends), I would say this country is more than 80% conservative. A lot more.

But hey, I guess Fox finds it necessary to give those atheist, flag-burning, baby-eating burnouts a forum. Because this is a free country. (Free to say stupid things, HA!)

Special Report with Bret Baier
One way to get a job at Fox News is to have a name where your first and last name begin with the same letter. And it's even better if that letter has a strong sounding syllable. Carl Cameron. Martha McCallum. Shepard Smith. Bret Baier.

Bret Bair has the show at 6pm, a crucial hour in the day. People are home from work (unless they're working a little extra to impress the boss that already left in time to watch The Five). And his show is called Special Report, meaning only the top news stories have made it this far. Like the upcoming NASCAR Sprint Chase for the Cup schedule. And how long Obama's latest costly vacation is.

For example, by this time of day, what was once a little nugget at Fox & Friends ("Is Obama an asshole?") is now a special top story with sourced quotes ("Obama is an asshole"), because people on Fox News (and web sites like Drudge and NewsMax) have been talking about it all day, building a wall of information that can't be denied and must therefore be called a "fact". Either the Obama administration must respond to these charges with transparent denials (thus proving the charge to those us who know better and who see through B. Hussein Obama's lies) or not say anything at all (thus proving the charge by remaining silent).

So Bret Baier has a lot of pressure. Fortunately, Bair looks like an action figure, with that cute mushroom head of his propped on his half-neck, his strong jaw line with mandibles able to chew a Wrigley's Juicy Juice into dust. His facade never cracks. He is oak, delivering his special report with total seriousness.

FOX Report with Shepard Smith

What the hell is this guy doing back? Twice in a day? And at 7pm? That's a crucial time slot too! The older viewers are almost in bed, so this is the last thing they watch, leaving them with Shep's liberal blasphemes to put them to sleep. Then this gets into their subconscious, and they wake up the next day as liberal zombies looking to eat some brains and score some meth.

And get this: Shep may not even pick up the Special Report handed to him on a silver platter by Bret Baier. Suddenly this "Obama is an asshole" story, which is national news (being picked up by the Washington Times, Media Research Center, and Rupert Murdoch's wife's book club) is suddenly stopped in its tracks if Shep decides NOT TO TALK ABOUT IT. Sure, there might be some bombing in Mumbai, a stock market crash, or some tainted meat that's in all our intestines. But I find it hard to believe he can't save that other crap for the last 15 minutes to tell us more about the "Obama is an asshole" scandal. By now Carl Cameron has been hitting the streets, getting quotes from his White House sources, the biggest bombshell of all being what Shep can lead with:

"Obama Administration denies that Obama is an asshole."

See? That's an admission right there! Or at least it *feels* like an admission. Why did he have to deny something unless it had some truth to it? Carl wouldn't have asked about it otherwise. It's not like someone is pulling his strings.

So anyway, Shep gets two chances a day to screw up everything Fox News is trying to say. He's a brick wall standing in the way of the news I want to hear.

The O'Reilly Factor ("The Factor®™©)
No one benefitted more from Bill Clinton's blowjob than Bill O'Reilly (though for about 30 seconds Bubba probably benefited from it too.).

Back in 1998, Bill O'Reilly was just your average former host of the Polk-Award-winning "Inside Edition" with a start-up show on Fox News. And back in 1998, that start-up show of his stuck with the Clinton scandal story every night, without letting up. And because he was giving people what they wanted to hear (real news, about blowjobs and cigars, concerning a president they didn't like), the ratings piled up, and a new concept was born: Primetime news where people could yell at each other, with Bill as a yelling moderator. And all the yelling was essential, because the age of his average viewer is 81. And they're stubborn in their refusal to turn on their hearing aids.

Bill isn't afraid to, as he puts it, "tell it like it is." I like that, except for the times when I disagree with him. Some people may not be able to handle the truth he dishes out, but man up, people! Bill doesn't want us to be a nation of crybabies. That's why I like to hear him complain and bitch at length about every little thing.

His Talking Points Memos are the centerpiece to his show. And they're quite easy to follow along. On the off chance he may talk too fast or say some Ivy-League words, everything he says goes up on screen too, so we can follow along. He thinks that highly of us (to know we want to follow along by reading) and he thinks that highly of his opinions (that he doesn't want us to miss anything he has to say).

And I love, love, love his idea of No Spin. He's got the balls to ask the tough questions that need to be answered. Like directly asking Obama, point-blank, "Why are you such an asshole?" Bill keeps people from answering any question except the one he asked. You can't change the subject on Bill. He'll cut off your mic, and call you a "pinhead." Being called "pinhead" by Bill is like being declared "Hellbound" by God. It is just that bad. Seriously, it's a fate worse than death by power drill.

Bill also revolutionized the way people interact on a news show, namely during a debate or panel discussion. He utilizes splitscreen technology to bring more people in on the conversation. This splitscreen approach lets him, a guest from the left (usually some doofus) and a person from the right (always smart and well-spoken to the point you're not sure what he's saying, but it sounds good so you go with it) discuss topics in a civil way (no guns allowed).

Now in the old days (1997), this type of debate was done in an orderly process, where a question was asked, one person would answer, the other guest would respond to that, the host would ask a follow up. It was all very cordial. And boring.

Bill changed all that. A new game was afoot. Bill would ask the question, and it became a Hunger Games free for all. Guest 1 would say a sentence, Guest 2 would interrupt while Guest 1 kept talking, and after a few seconds, Bill would shout over them. It was awesome! It finally proved what we had all learned on the playground years ago: that shouting was the way to get your point across. And whoever yells the loudest wins. And we can all thank Bill O'Reilly for that. THANK YOU!!!!!!!

However, sometimes a liberal may come on the show and something he says gets through the cacophony. This is bad news, because that's not supposed to happen anywhere, especially on Fox News. For example, during a panel discussion some liberal might say that non-violent pot users shouldn't go to jail (!), and this would save millions in tax dollars every year. This is scary stuff. Because once this is said, on live TV, it can't be taken back. You can't unring the bell. But Bill can. He knows instantly that we have a problem. And he nimbly takes charge and bravely solves it by... going to commercial. We come back from break, and that liberal is gone. Bill then pulls out the "P" card, calling the recently departed guest a "Pinhead" (oh yeah, he went there!), and saying that The Factor®™ doesn't stand for that kind of thing. It's a classy show, with occasional updates on Jamie Lynn Spears' pregnancy.

Bill also revolutionized something else. The interview. In fact, he sometimes calls his interviews The Interview®. Because they're so much better than any other interview. Other interviews are just crap!

But that's not the big thing. In the old days, there would be an interview (think 60 Minutes), and then they would go on to the next story. And that was that. Interview over. The viewer is forced to base his opinion of what he saw, without added context or commentary. That's ridiculous!

Bill changed all that. Now when he does a big Interview, it's on tape. And when a segment (or the whole Interview) is over, we go back to the studio where Bill and a blond friend of his (Monica Crowley or Liz Cheney or Glenn Beck) discuss what they just saw. For example, if the interview was with George W. Bush, the main topic of conversation is "awesomeness". Much discussion centers around how awesome Bush spoke, how awesome his ideas are, how he stands up for those ideas, how good looking he is, how he jogs 60 miles a day, how he farms 400 acres by himself. This way the viewer gets added insight from the interview, a lot more than from just the interview itself. And if Bush happened to say something so controversial during the interview ("Which one was Saddam Hussein again?") that it created a national backlash, Bill is there to let us know IT WASN'T THAT BAD.

Meanwhile, if the interview was with Obama, the discussion is rightly about "assholeness," how Obama is all arrogant and uppity (but not in a racist way), how he plans bombings with Bill Ayers, wrote Pastor Jeremiah Wright's sermons, and hates America. This added insight really helps me see the interview in a new way. Because while I may have watched it and thought, "Maybe Obama makes some good points," the discussion that follows proves that my thinking was way off. It's the same with the Bush interview. I may think, "Bush isn't making much sense here. I'm not sure he knows what he's talking about." But the post-interview discussion shows me that Bush actually thinks on a higher plane than the rest of us, so if what he says doesn't make sense to us, it's OUR fault.

Also, Bill made it OK to be a real dick on TV.

Hannity

You don't have time to catch your breath after The Factor. Because Hannity comes on at 9. But you don't call it Hannity. It needs more oomph and pizzazz and balls. It's more like *Hannity*! Or ***HANNITY!***

I like Sean Hannity... sometimes. I'm really glad he got rid of Alan "Skeletor" Colmes. What I liked about the old version of the show (Hannity & Colmes) isn't that it showed two opposing points of view (who needs that?). No, what I liked had more to do with how Sean Hannity looked. Because in Sean Hannity we had a visual composite that reflects how conservatives see themselves: as photogenic, smart, dark-haired, always right, charming and quick with an answer. And that in Alan Colmes, it had a composite that reflected how conservatives see liberals: as freaky looking.

When the time came for Colmes to leave, I shared a collective, simultaneous thought with other Fox News viewers: "It's about time." Then we wondered "Who will replace him?" The answer: nobody. *That* was brilliant. What was once a show with a conservative and liberal arguing against one another (with Hannity only getting 75% of the airtime), became a show about a conservative arguing against nobody. In fact, it was a way for Hannity to be THE MAN, who invited like-minded folks on his show to talk about how bad liberals are (a discussion topic without end) and to get occasional guest Sarah Palin all riled up in her sexy Hockey Mom way. You and me, Sarah Barracuda, let's face off up against the glass and get puckin'. (Note to self: Edit this part out before publication).

Though I still don't know why, instead of having him leave the show, he didn't just shoot Colmes in the face. He had it coming. He was a liberal. (I'm kidding, of course. Unless you don't want me to be kidding).

29

When it comes to interviews, Hannity is the go-to guy for conservatives in trouble. He's like a one-man group home. A Dr. Phil without any of the scolding but with a lot more hair. For example, if the liberal media claims that a married conservative politician was caught boinking a nun in the confessional at St. Patrick's Cathedral (based only on sworn testimony, videotape evidence and matching DNA of the child that resulted from it), Hannity will interview that politician with tough questions like, "Are your opponents attacking because you're a Christian?" and "What 10 amazing things about you doesn't the public know?" and "Founding Father Thomas Jefferson had an affair, too. Do you see yourself as the next Thomas Jefferson? Because I do."

On the Record with Greta
I'm not up this late watching TV. It's 10 o'clock, people! Get to bed! Plus studies say adults need eight hours of sleep per night, and the only way to do that and still wake up for Fox & Friends is to be asleep by 10. It's a Sophie's Choice-like decision: Greta, first hour of F&F, or 8 hours of sleep? Pick two.

CHAPTER 5
CNN: Extremists

As far as anyone can tell, CNN was the world's first 24-hour cable news network. It began in 1979, but no one really noticed it existed until 1991, during the first Iraq War. Before then, it was a channel you flipped past on your way to MTV or some pixelated porn.

But thanks to Saddam Hussein invading Kuwait, CNN started to matter. People started to care about the news at times other than 6 and 11pm. In fact, CNN became so big that it added a station, Headline News. So now CNN is stuck with TWO cable news stations that no one watches.

This is a very tough chapter for me to write. Mainly because I don't watch CNN. That's right. I'm part of the 99%.

The 99% of the country that doesn't watch CNN.

So I have a choice if I want to finish writing this book in three days: Watch CNN all day long, take notes, analyze what I see and write it all down. Or just go by what I've gleaned from online banner ads for CNN and a quick Wikipedia read. To the Internet!

American Morning

Imagine "Morning Joe" or "Fox & Friends", but without the playful conversation and flirting. Also, imagine that no host stays on the show for longer than two months. That's "American Morning." More people have hosted this show than have played professional baseball. I think I even hosted this show once and never even knew about it. A Wikipedia search tells me that American Morning is now hosted by a group of ladies with names that sound more like sleep medication: Ashleigh Banfield, Zoraida Sambolin and Soledad O'Brien. It's like "The View", only more newsy, and less Whoopi-y.

Unlike a lot of CNN shows, which get cancelled and replaced on a regular basis, "American Morning" has been going strong for 10 years. It's one area of stability on CNN.

UPDATE:

American Morning has been cancelled and was replaced with "Early Start" and "Starting Point." (It's only a matter of time before they add "Early Point"). But Banfield, Sambolin and O'Brien remain.

CNN Newsroom

This is news every hour featuring a new anchor, hosted by ladies that are as interchangeable as Legos. Kyra, Suzanne, Randi, Brooke. Each hour has a new host! It's like they're auditioning... FOR ME! And I can judge them like Hugh Hefner. And since they're each delivering the same news stories each hour, I don't really have to listen to what they're saying (All the good stuff is at the bottom crawl anyway). You can just watch to see how they say it. And how they look while doing so. Then when it's over, I can judge their performance.

31

The Situation Room

The Situation here is that the show is four hours too long. Wolf Blitzer stands in a high-tech room like some Bond villain, sashaying from one big screen to another, as CNN reporters show up bigger than life on those screens, giving him the Situation. Wolf holds a clipboard. And wears a dark suit. And glasses. And dark shoes. And has a beard.

[NOTE: I don't watch this show. All I know comes from a still image I saw on the Internet].

But from what I think I know, an old curmudgeon named Jack Cafferty shows up every once in awhile to make Wolf Blitzer look young and to complain. He *is* an old man after all. What else is he gonna do?

Cafferty is an old school journalist; at one time he mentored Edward R. Murrow. But with age comes wisdom. And anger. Lots and lots of anger. I think the reason he's kept off Wolf's set is because the producers are afraid Cafferty will rip Wolf's beard off and feed it to him.

John King Has a Show!

John King might be Larry King's son… no one knows for sure. Regardless, John King leveraged his unmatched talent with a Smartboard® last election season into getting his own show. And when you talk about John King, you must always refer to him as John King. Nothing else makes sense. Even John King refers to himself as "John King."

Erin Burnett OutFront

Erin Burnett is the current CNN 7pm person. Between the moment I write this and the moment I take a break to take a dump, her show may very well be cancelled. The book-writing industry moves too slow to keep up with the revolving door that is 7pm on CNN. Twitter moves too slow for it, too.

I won't spend too much time writing about this… don't want to waste the effort for a show that may not have much of a half-life… but I promise to write a full-page on it in the updated version of this book, "Obama is STILL a Big Stupid Poopy Pants."

Or maybe I can host the next show on at 7pm on CNN. *Mike Lawrence: AlmostCancelled.*

Piers Morgan

I miss Larry King. He was a throwback. To a time when the news was delivered via telegraph. He's the only journalist to have reported on the Kennedy *and* Lincoln assassinations. He was in the field when meteors killed the dinosaurs. He reported on the Big Bang. He transcribed for Moses. He's old.

Piers Morgan took over for Larry after what must have been an exhaustive search consisting of three or four candidates. They could have gone younger with Regis Philbin. But instead they went totally young and British with Piers Morgan. That's right… BRITISH! He's one of our enemies! I haven't buried the grudge from the Revolutionary War and the War of 1812, like some people. The Brits were our first enemy. And I don't want to get all cozy with them. This isn't like when Rocky and Apollo got all chummy after years of beating each other senseless. That was fiction! This is real life. And the Brits can suck it.

360 with Anderson

Why is this show called 360? Because that's how many hours per day Anderson Cooper is on TV.

He's everywhere. He's got a primetime show on CNN. A syndicated talk show (yeah, *he's* totally the next Oprah). And he even drops by "60 Minutes" (sometimes to do a news story, sometimes to say hi to his great-grandpa Morley Safer). And he hosts CNN's New Year's Eve show. This guy is the Ryan Seacrest of cable news.

And he brought a brand new idea to news, in the form of the RidicuLIST. That's right. While other news outlets are so serious all the time, Anderson thought it would be novel to point out the funny side of news. So thanks for that innovation, Anderson. If you can find a way to work in a weather report, you can be known as a true visionary.

CHAPTER 6
MSNBC: Rachel Maddow's gay. Need I say more?

Like North Korean state television was to Kim Jung Il, MSNBC is to Obama. It's the Obama News Network. I wish I had a network that spent 24 hours a day telling me how great I am. A network that kisses my ass and doesn't feel the least bit embarrassed about it. "Today on MSNBC: Obama's Greatness, Part 427: How He Invented Electricity and Won all the Super Bowls."

It's obvious the bosses at MSNBC don't respect the 20 members of their audience. Because they don't bring the hot looking pieces of ass to the anchor desk! Pop Quiz: How many former Miss America contestants does MSNBC have anchoring their news shows? Answer: NONE. Even if you come in 51st place in a pageant (assuming Puerto Rico is in the running), MSNBC doesn't want you, no matter how hard you said you'd fight to end world hunger. So beautiful girls need not apply. That's discrimination, people!

Now I won't spend too much time discussing this "news" "network". Unless I get off on a rant here. But getting off on a rant here is so 1993.

MSNBC is last in ratings (except they're quick to point out that Current TV is technically a news network, so MSNBC can claim to beat *somebody*). The only category where MSNBC comes out on top is letters in a name. Seriously, FIVE LETTERS? Sounds like a bit of "call letter envy." I thought ESPN was a long stick to swing around, but "MSNBC" won't even roll off Gene Simmons' tongue. MSNBC needs an abbreviation for its abbreviation! HA!

And what does MSNBC stand for? I can't confirm it, but sources say it's Mostly Stupid News By Cokeheads. However, this isn't entirely accurate. Because the network gets its news from Crackheads, as well.

Now we all know that MSNBC is the most liberal network in history of the world, and their sole purpose is to turn people into baby-eating, pot-chomping, slacker America-destroying, Obama slaves. It's a propaganda machine designed to cater to the whims of Alec Baldwin. And Bill Gates, apparently.

MSNBC tries to be a lot like Fox News, with various shows throughout the day that provide ample opportunity for talk radio hosts to show their faces on TV and speak loudly. Fox has it down to a science. When MSNBC does it, it's embarrassing. Also, they interview newspaper reporters instead of those radio hosts. Seriously, do I want my opinions from some dude pissing away his time in front of a typewriter at the Washington Post, or do I want my info from Barry "Buck Wild" Cherry of WNTY's Morning Zoo?

What can you expect from MSNBC on a weekday? A lot of liberal claptrap. What can you expect on the weekend? Prison shows. Lots and lots of prison shows. But let's first look at what's showing on the weekdays.

Morning Joe
I love the title of this show, because it has a subtle double meaning. One, because the host's name is Joe. And second, it's on in the morning. Pretty clever. Though I'm not sure what the coffee stain logo has to do with anything.

MJ is hosted by Joe Scarborough, a former Republican Congressman from Florida. He's what some conservatives call "Republican-lite" or "RINO" or "Judas Iscariot." The fact that he's on a liberal propaganda machine masquerading as a news network tells you he's been brainwashed. I think this brainwashing is so severe that he can't even see clearly. Some days he wears glasses, some days he doesn't. What's up with that?

This is one of those "relaxed" shows, with people around a round table having a roundtable discussion. Mika Brezenyskyvisky (sp?) delivers the news, often providing excerpts from the country's four remaining newspapers that still have a print edition. Mika is pretty in the way an ice-cold assassin sent to kill James Bond is pretty. And she's pretty in that her name is Mika, which is just so much fun to say. If her name was Gertrude, she might not be as cute. Anyway, her main role is to read news excerpts, which in turn allows the boys to react.

The boys include Joe, Willie Geist, who looks like a young punk with a face you'd love to rub in quicksand, and a couple old guys who write for Boston newspapers or host unwatched shows on CNBC. The one rule for the boys is not to be more entertaining or sound smarter than Joe. Which means having the personality and facial animation of a statue. And they succeed admirably. It's the one morning show that actually tries to put its audience back to sleep so early in the morning. It's a televised snooze alarm. Joe Scarboring. However, one thing that shows Joe's superiority over Obama is that he never uses a teleprompter. Because Joe has an opinion on everything! And it's a detailed opinion, too. One time I saw him talk the whole three hours without taking a break. And when the show came on the next day, he was still going strong, having filibustered through the night without stopping. I'd never heard such an insightful and extended commentary on U by Kotex® tampons.

Andrea Mitchell Reports
I'm not sure what's on after Morning Joe, and quite frankly, I don't even feel like taking 30 seconds to find out on the MSNBC homepage. Plus when you log on to their site they use subliminal messaging to brainwash you (Yvan eht nioj).

However, at some point in the early afternoon, a show with Andrea Mitchell comes on. It's called "Andrea Mitchell Reports". It's a mix between a news show, interview show, and analysis. Yeah, I know. I don't get it either.

Andrea is like Barbara Walters, in that she's an old-school female journalist, but without the mountain of success. Which must really piss her off. Andrea is part of the Holy Trinity of pioneering female TV reporters from the 1970s. Diane Sawyer. Barbara Walters. And Andrea Mitchell. Diane Sawyer was the Michael Corleone of the group, sensible but ruthless when she has to be. Barbara Walters was like Sonny, headstrong but asked too many questions. And Andrea Mitchell is like Fredo, who was sent away to a fledgling desert wasteland.

I think of "Andrea Mitchell Reports" as a bridge between the "moderate" Joe Scarborough and the "radical" shows (Sharpton, Schultz, Madcow) that follow. It's MSNBC's way of boiling the frog, gradually getting you into their brownshirt army of liberal ideas and turning you into a machine bent on killing America. Sure, Morning Joe may seem harmless and at times rational, but try it once and you may become addicted. To stupid ideas!

Sure, Andrea skews to the left, but she doesn't veer off into the Planet Xenon with ridiculous talk of progressive taxes and workplace safety. Nope, she's a longtime professional, and she knows how to make you, the viewer, think you're watching some unbiased reporting. I, of course, know that she's truly a Marxist. But how are you going to tell? By the time her show is over and you start to think, "Hey, this lady may be a commie," you're suddenly watching Al Sharpton's show, and the shock of what he has to say makes you forget all about her.

Also, Andrea Mitchell looks refreshing young for someone who's 65. And sleeping with Alan Greenspan.

Dylan Ratigan
I'm not sure who he is or even if he still has a show. But I'm sure he craves any kind of attention. So here it is.

His name sounds made up, like it's some muppet from Fraggle Rock. From what I think I know, he's their financial expert, a Neil Cavuto without the charismatic sexual power known as the Cavuto Seduction.

I'm going to assume that like all MSNBC hosts, he's been suspended. Or cancelled.

The Al Sharpton Happy Fun Time Hour
So they did it. They gave Al Sharpton a TV show. The Apocalypse is nearly complete. All that's left is for Demi Moore to die in childbirth and reboot the Guf.

Is it me, or does Al look a lot smaller on TV than in real life? I thought the camera was supposed to add 10 lbs. But this guy looks like an adult My Buddy doll.

Al adds a bit of color to MSNBC's lineup. Now by color, I don't mean he's black. I mean he's suspicious, high-fallutin, sneaky, loudmouthed, threatening, angry, doesn't know his place, uppity, and descended from slaves. Now I'm sure some crazy liberals would say those phrases are "code" words that racists use, a sort of wink and nudge that gives tacit permission and acceptance of bigoted and discriminatory attitudes. Heh heh, that's just way off base!! There are no codewords, and racism has been gone since Obama took office.

20 8 5 25' 18 5

15 14

20 15

21 19!

Moving right along... Al does something that's really annoying. He doesn't ask Yes or No questions. Or long meandering questions that give respondents an "out", where they take one part of the question and answer THAT. Instead, he demands answers, and will ask follow-ups. And because he's a preacher, he does it with flair and eloquence and clever use of syntax. I hate that! It's not fair that he bases his arguments on sound reasoning and a gift for vocabulary. How are his interview subject supposed to stand up to that?

Hardball with Chris Matthews
Chris Matthews loves to talk. When he speaks it feels like it's in ALL CAPS. His is the only show where the questions always go on longer than the answers. Sometimes a question runs for two segments, interrupted by a commercial break.

Chris calls his show "Hardball" because he asks the tough questions. Maybe the questions would be easier if he limited them to less than 1,200 words. Dinner at the Olive Garden (waiting in line included) doesn't take as long as one of his questions.

To me, the funniest part of his show is the last segment, which is called "Let me finish...". I only wish he would.

It's called "Hardball" because it symbolizes the lengthy process where a lump of coal, through centuries of time and pressure, becomes a diamond. Which is also a process that takes half as long as a question asked by Chris Matthews.

He wrote a biography on Jack Kennedy. It's one sentence spanning 1,500 pages. And is the first of eight parts. John F. Kennedy lived to be 46. It'll take twice that long to read this book.

One time Chris Matthews went to Denny's for breakfast. By the time he was done ordering, it was dinnertime.

It takes Chris Matthews two hours to say, "Have a nice day."

When Chris Matthews recites the Gettysburg Address, it really does take four score and seven years.

Chris Matthews' outgoing voicemail message runs longer than Ken Burns' "Baseball."

By the time Chris Matthews was done seducing a teenager, she was 65.

In conclusion, Chris Matthews talks a lot.

The Ed Show
Ed Schultz is the one guy who truly looks like his voice.

Back when he just had his radio show, and whenever I happened to hear it flipping between Hannity and Prager, I imagined this slightly overweight guy in his early 50s, with brown hair combed back, a slightly rubbery face, some squinty eyes. Then he got on TV and he lived up to my imagination.

Ed's show is called "The Ed Show". No last names necessary. Because Schultz sounds foreign. *And because he's just a regular guy like you and me.* (sarcasm in italics.). Except that he has his own TV show! And we all know that everyone on TV is a famous celebrity who lives like a king in gold-plated mansions that have swimming pools filled with Dom Perignon Crystal Corbel Franzia Champagne. So this "I'm an everyman" shtick doesn't really play to the masses. We're not fooled Ed*ward Schultz*.

But Ed still claims to speak up for the blue-collar guy. But then he supports Barack "Liberal East Coast Elite" Obama over the likes of John "Blue Collar Ohio" Boehner. How do I know Boehner is more rugged than Obama? Because Boehner still smokes! Just like real Americans! The men and women who built this country smoked like chimneys, and their descendants didn't let a little thing like a Surgeon's General Warning or emphysema or birth defects or bad breath or yellow teeth or a foul stench coming out of their pores or mucus constantly running up and down their windpipes stop them from smoking and looking oh so cool while doing it. Watch an old movie with Robert Mitchum smoking, and just try to not pick up the habit.

If Ed really did support the blue-collar worker, why doesn't he take some of the billions he's made from his TV show and give that money away to his working buddies? Suddenly distributing the wealth isn't so great when it's your wealth being distributed!

The highlight of Ed's show is his Question of the Day. You see, Ed starts his show with a long monologue about how bad Republicans are. Then he asks a question that feels just a *bit one-sided*.

Who's to blame for my haircut: Republicans or Democrats?

Should we end tax cuts for the rich Republicans? Yes or No?

Do you think kidnapping is bad? Yes or No?

Would you like it if A Republican sandpapered your scrotum? Yes or No?

I think the goal of these questions is to get a unanimous verdict. Because all liberals think alike anyway. They're just sheep, reacting to the talking pinheads in front of them.

Now to buy some gold before Goldline runs out.

The Rachel Maddow Show
So here we are. Maddow. My mortal enemy. The Neo of liberal pundits. The One. The One I Want To Be Rid Of. The one who drives me crazy with her seeming intelligence and *niceness*. She who shall not be named.

Rachel Maddow.

Why does she have to be so nice?

And what's with all the smiling? Doesn't she know that anger is what sells? That it's anger and volume that makes the case? Is she trying to be different so she stands out, or stands above the fray? Where's the fun in that? Maybe she's using humor as a defense mechanism, because she knows at the end of the day she's defending a stupid poopy pants president, and the only way she can live with herself is to smile. Like the Joker.

Her hero is Keith Olbermann, so this part about her is my own Special Comment, as if Keith himself would say it:

Every morning I wake up with hope, hope that this country can be great again, to become the beacon of light that once illuminated innovation, brought forth inspiration, and set forth ideation. I want that illumination to shine through today and beyond.

It was Neville Chamberlain who once said, upon reaching a decisive victory against the proletariat masses in that maelstrom of the winter that was 1943, "A great nation is made great by its greatness." And it is in this vein that We the People embark on a daily pilgrimage to achieve greatness, bit by bit, step by excruciating step.

Ms. Maddow, how dare you quash our greatness with your unflagging determination to undermine this nation and send us all on a course of pestilence, disease and famine! Your diatribes against our great leaders weaken us all, like when you called John Kyl out for once saying "What I said on the Senate floor was not meant to be taken as a factual statement." For giving Ezra Klein a forum with which to speak. And for being so tall while Sean Hannity challenges himself vertically? Have you no shame, madam?

It's like you don't even care. You rule your show with an iron, man-sized fist. You make your viewers worship at your Cisco-Telepresence alter, calling upon them to sacrifice reason and common sense and their beliefs in God as you rework their way of thinking, creating an army of Maddowbots who seek to usurp the democracy that made you successful.

41

Children are watching, Ms. Maddow. They watch, and listen, and they imitate. They're the innocent victims in all this, the ones too meek to defend themselves against your onslaught, as you catapult a way of thinking that tears apart the very fabric of our republic. Do you want those children to be like you? Nearsighted, talkative, gay, liberal and tall?

What is your motive, Ms. Maddow? What is it you want? What is your RANSOM?

Is it all-consuming power you seek? A Godlike ability to bend us to your will? Free beer?

Well I for one say you can be stopped. You must be stopped. Otherwise we all suffer in the hell you've created for us, as we burn down to our soul, holding on to our last bit of purity as you attempt to cast from us all that make us good. And in the ruin that is left, you will thrust your darkness upon the sea of flames and earth of dust, a darkness of death and damnation where not even the maggots and cockroaches that feast on your bones would dare to tread.

To see the complete 45-minute version of this Special Comment, go to OlbermannBlows.geocities.com.

The Last Word with Lawrenzzzzz O' Donnell
This guy is dangerous. My advice to you... don't leave the iron on during his show. Because you'll wake up with your house burnt to the ground. And the last thing you'll remember hearing before you slumbered off, "And today the do-nothing Republicans outdid themselves by doing even less."

Now I'm a huge fan of small, nearly non-existent government. But I will make an exception for a federal highway safety law against Lawrence doing any narration for books on tape for fear people in cars may listen, doze off and kill us all.

They say Lawrence's show is an hour long. If that's true, then if I'm ever on death row, let my last hour be one where I watch The Last Word, so my final moments feel like years.

Lawrence used to be a Congressman, where even C-SPAN cut away to an empty chair and turned the sound down when he spoke, to give the audience something a little more exciting.

Because Lawrence is boring, it makes sense that we have no reason to listen to what he has to say. Sure he may come armed with facts when he interviews a conservative on his show, and he's very well-prepared in his "Re-write" portion of the show, but guess what? We ain't listening. Your soothing voice may work on the grandkids when you read them to bed, but on us, we're just flipping to watch Greta. Or "Man vs. Food."

Weekends On MSNBC

On the weekends MSNBC goes from being a liberal bastion of talking heads and Cisco Telepresence interviews to a network that's all about prisons. It's quite an abrupt change. Friday night at 9:59 Maddow is raging in her smiley way about attacks on her precious unions (oh boo hoo), but at 10pm, we flip to a beast with tattoos all over his body, piercings through his face, and low angle cameras in prison cells. We get it. Prison sucks. Thanks for the news flash. Maybe MSNBC can also devote some time uncovering the truth behind the Sun: that it's hot.

However, if the point of all these prison shows is to scare people straight, then they don't go far enough. MSNBC needs to graphically show the prison rapes, the stabbings, the beatings, and the humiliation of taking a dump in front of your roommate. A roommate who giggles at EVERYTHING.

But MSNBC won't go there. Too afraid to report the truth. So by not showing the whole story at prisons (the good and the bad), they're actually shirking their journalistic responsibility. And if MSNBC holds back on the weekends, imagine what they hold back during the week. They're not to be trusted.

CHAPTER 7
My solution: the All-Speculation News Network (ASNN)

So the 24-hour news networks just don't cut it. We need to change the status quo in the way we receive our news (via television). And that solution is the All-Speculation News Network (ASNN).

The ASNN would have a simple motto: No facts. Just speculation.

It's a motto to live by. And that motto makes it a lot easier to fill the 24-hour-long gaps in the 24-hour-long news cycle.

Why would an-all speculation news network work so well? Let me set the stage:

At 10am on a clear blue Tuesday, a building collapses in Detroit. Suddenly, this is the biggest news story of the day. Even bigger than Angelina Jolie losing 5 lbs.

Now your average news network feels an obligation to report the facts. But in this case, I just gave you all the facts. "Building fell down. In Detroit." That took about three seconds. Unfortunately, a story this big has hours of airtime to fill. People want to know WHAT IS GOING ON! Because the building collapse is now the STORY OF THE DAY, we can't really report on anything else. We can't cut away to a pre-produced story on some old couple reuniting 50 years after they were high school sweethearts. People want to hear about the collapse. They're hungry for details. That old couple can piss off!

But...

We don't have anything else to tell them. The extent of our facts is out there. Building fell down. In Detroit. Sure we have reporters on the scene, we're on the phone with cops and fire departments in Detroit, we sent emails to our contacts in the city government, we flipped through the white pages and randomly called Detroit residents, hoping to fall ass-backwards into a witness. But all that stuff TAKES TIME.

Meanwhile the anchors are forced to just repeat themselves and work without a script. It's uncomfortable to watch. They're not trained for this sort of thing.

To alleviate this, your standard news network will fill the time by finding a reporter to speak to, because he's "out in the field". Or he's "on his way to the field." Or he's "fucking lost." So the reporter talks on his cellphone, and instead of actually seeing him talk, we get a picture of him, and a grabber of a theme graphic, perhaps with some wordplay (like "Motor City Madness" or "Detroit Rocked City"). And the phone reception is bad. And he has nothing new to say, and you can just feel the tension in his voice.... He wants to give us some new info. It's just not happening. Because he's constrained by the facts. His journalistic integrity prevents him from saying anything else. Because if he's wrong, his fellow reporters will laugh at him over drinks later.

But what if he didn't have to be constrained by these facts? What if our anchors and reporters and on-camera guests could speculate to their heart's content, with no limits or boundaries on what they could say? What if, when that building falls in Detroit, the anchors could banter a bit, and give their own assessments... educated guesses based on their experience? It might go a little something like this:

Judd: And this just in. A building in Detroit has collapsed.
Sheila: Any reports on casualties?
Judd: (looking at the paper in front of him) No.
Sheila: I bet it's a lot.
Judd: I don't want to manipulate the audience's emotions, but maybe there were children in that building.
Sheila: And the ones that perished are the lucky ones, as others are trapped in what could be an agonizing week of unanswered hope, despair and loss before the sweet release of death ends their excruciating pain.
Judd: Well said, Sheila. It was probably terrorists.
Sheila: Probably? How about likely! We've been long overdue for an attack.
Judd: And Detroit makes a great target. Because we got the auto industry there. And the resurgent Lions.
Sheila: That's right. They'd be attacking our vehicular infrastructure, and be destroying the backbone of this nation as they break up the Matthew Stafford to Calvin Johnson connection.
Judd: Who knows? Maybe this is the first of a string of bombings. Any building could be next. Or maybe a house. Your

45

house. [Judd looks directly at the camera and points menacingly]

Sheila: I think people should start to panic.

Judd: Absolutely. Perhaps even evacuate the city. Though it may already be too late.

Sheila: Hold on! We have a reporter at the scene. Let's go to Carson Ricardo on the Subway Eat Fresh Conoco Phillips Hotline sponsored by Zales, the Galleria of Jewelry. Carson, what do you know?

Carson: Not a whole lot, Sheila. The cops have the area blocked off, and I dropped my notepads with my questions on them. But I can tell you that there's a lot of dust in the air. Like maybe the building wasn't very clean.

Judd: Could that be because lazy illegals were part of the cleaning crew?

Carson: I don't see why not.

Sheila: What kind of building was it, Carson?

Carson: A tall one. I think. It's hard to tell since it's all rubble now.

Sheila: Is it downtown? Where are you?

Carson: I'm not sure. I had just typed in the address in my Tom Tom, and it got me here.

Judd: Are there any landmarks? Like Joe Louis's arm?

Carson: Nope. Let me ask around. Hey! Where are we?

Voice from off camera: You're in Detroit, stupidass!

Later on, after the banter between anchor and reporter has reached its conclusion (at least until we once again "go back to Carson for the latest at the scene") we would call in some "experts." Since I want the speculation to be fixed around the idea of "terrorism" (it *is* the best guess at the time, and fear is good for ratings. Nobody's flipping to "Wheel of Fortune" if we have teasers saying, "And we have information that reveals where the terrorist may strike next. After the break."), I'll be sure to get some guys from the American Enterprise Institute or Heritage Foundation or John Bolton or some "string 'em up sheriff" from Arizona or a radio DJ wearing a flag-patterned jacket. For example, a discussion with John Bolton and the DJ would go like this:

Judd: Mr. Bolton, thanks for being here with us.

Bolton: Thank you. We must destroy the United Nations.

Judd: You've been an expert for decades on this sort of thing. Can we definitively say it's the work of terrorists?

Bolton: Yes. It was Muslim terrorists emboldened by the fact we have a UN. Let's just burn the building to the ground. Today. Don't even evacuate the sumbitch.

Radio DJ, interjecting: Maybe if Michelle "AllDrama" would stop telling us what to eat, we could avoid these terrorist attacks altogether, am I right?

Judd: So what's the president's next step? Is it time to unleash nuclear weapons?

Bolton: The best defense is a great offence. And the best offense is an attack that decimates your enemy's defenses. And burns off their skin. Look, I've got the explosives, the gasoline, and a way in. We could turn the UN building into a pile of rubble within two hours. It'll be like the end of "Fight Club." Who's with me?

DJ: Where is the birth certificate? My listeners want to know! I've worn this American flag T-shirt for 15 straight days now! It's my version of a Hunger Strike. Follow me on Twitter! Someone invite me to Pinterest!

This would continue for 30 minutes.

Either way, whatever the truth is behind that building collapse, I would spend a lot of time (before that truth comes out) speculating that terrorists and liberals were behind it. Because if we're right, then we're the network that brought you the truth FIRST. (Scoop!) But if we're wrong, so what? We'd have still educated viewers on the dangers of liberalism, and connected that liberalism with terrorism. If we pound that message into the audience's heads enough, then we'll have done our part for America. Let's face it. Liberals are bad. Horrible. Like terrorists, they want to destroy America. So if my news network can provide a forum where we bash those liberals in, we're doing the country a favor. It's like Charles Manson. Most people never witnessed him kill anybody. But we all know he's evil. So maybe we haven't seen liberals plot a terrorist attack, or eat one of our babies, but everyone needs to know how inherently shitty they are.

The ASNN would do that. And never be boring. The world is an exciting place. So why make its news so lame?

CHAPTER 8
Jon Stewart: He just pisses me off

Jon Stewart, how do I hate thee? Let me count the ways.

First off, I did some digging (Wikipedia-style, print edition… boy did that cost a lot!), and he is not a journalist. He doesn't even have a journalism background! Jon Stewart was a comedian, and judging by his "performance" in the box office flop "The Faculty" (ANOTHER movie that shows how bad unionized teachers can be), he's an "actor" too. Typical Hollywood liberal.

But I guess that's just how Comedy Central does news. They don't take it seriously.

Second, Stewart treats his news show like a big joke. At least that's what I think. I don't find it funny but his audience (probably high on weed) laughs at everything he says. Maybe they're laughing at his big nose.

Third, I don't like the way he uses recorded video footage to show the hypocrisy of public officials, especially conservatives. I'm sure that in some ways, unedited and unaltered footage of a conservative saying one thing, and then later saying the exact opposite could be construed as "hypocrisy." But I'm sure there could be a rational explanation. Maybe it was "Opposite Day" in Congress that day. Maybe the senator was cloned. Maybe the other footage was from an alternate universe. Did Jon Stewart ever think of that? No! He just jumps to the conclusions supplied by the videotape! Maybe if he dug a little deeper he would get to the truth. But like I said, he's no journalist.

Fourth, he asks tough questions, and even asks follow-ups to his guests. Doesn't he realize they're there to promote something? Let Newt Gingrich talk about his book! Quit asking about that account at Tiffany's! Quit making the point that a fiscal conservative spending $500,000 on jewelry is the height of hypocrisy. Now I have to pause the show, go to some online message boards, and find out why Newt's Tiffany's account is no big deal. Dammit!

I have this sneaking feeling that instead of just "winging it", Stewart actually prepares his questions ahead of time, anticipates an answer and has a question ready for that. It's bullshit. I'm all for that kind of work ethic, but not when it's used to catapult the liberal propaganda!

However, there are parts of the Daily Show I like. About once a month, Jon Stewart turns the tables on Obama, showing the president's own hypocrisy. But I don't think Jon's heart is really in it. This "Obama-bashing" on his part just his way of saying, "Hey, we go after both sides. Don't call us unfair." It's a cover story. If he really wanted to take down Obama, why not mention *his* Tiffany's account? I just know Obama has a diamond-studded necklace that reads "WHITE HOUSE THUG", and you can only get those at Tiffany's. At least when Newt shops there, it's for his wife. Because he's a loving husband. Just ask any woman.

CHAPTER 9
Where the hell is the flag lapel pin?

Every president since George W. Bush has worn an American flag lapel pin on a regular basis. Every president that is, except Obama!

There's only one conclusion to be drawn from this. Obama is no patriot. He hates America. (OK, that's two conclusions, but they're kind of related).

Now back when he was running for president, Obama said his patriotism doesn't come from wearing a lapel pin, but from the way he acts. (I didn't know he was a comedian.). Man he sorely misjudged the American people! When it comes to patriotism, we demand visual evidence, especially from Democrats and liberals. And then we dismiss it.

But Obama learned pretty damn quick. Now he always wears a flag lapel pin. And this just makes him a hypocrite! So not only is he an America-hater, but he also sold out on his beliefs! What a flip-flopper. Now instead of despising him for not wearing a pin, I can despise him for choosing to do so. It's a win-win.

The lapel pin flap displays one of the strengths of conservatives. We base a lot of our opinions on emotion and on things others may see as insignificant. Liberals may say, "It's just a lapel pin. Get over it." Saying something like that just makes liberals insignificant (HA!). "Just a lapel pin?" Um, it has the flag on it. The U.S. flag. And just because it's small doesn't mean it doesn't matter. My eyeballs are small. But I don't want to be without them!

And while we're on Obama's patriotism, what's with the way he grabs his crotch when the National Anthem is being played? I know you know which YouTube video I'm talking about. I have always, always, always (ever since it became the norm after 9/11 and everyone else started doing it) put my hand on my heart when the National Anthem is played. That shows you're serious. That you love America. That you love going to the ballgame. Obama, meanwhile, was caught holding his junk (look at the pictures!) during "The Star Spangled Banner." More like "Ball-Dangled Manner" HA! Obama's arms are just hanging down, his hands folded in front of his balls. Is that any way to stand?

Now I first saw that ball-grabbing picture from an email a friend sent me. I get lots of emails from friends, and some of the stuff they have in there are SHOCKING. (My favorite emails are the ones with lots and lots of claims about how bad Obama is. Those litanies against Obama... he's BFFs with Williams Ayers, he has pro-choice people as advisors, he wants sex ed taught to pre-schoolers... really add up). Now liberals may say these emails are hoaxes, or the claims are exaggerated or misguided or totally wrong. But liberals are stupid. Why believe them?

Cases in point:

• While I see the idea of Obama having a pro-choice advisor as scary, a liberal may say that it's only proof that Obama prefers his advisors to be Democrats.

• While I think Obama wants to hand out copies of the Kama Sutra to kindergarten classes and teach 5-year-olds a bunch of gay sex moves, a liberal will claim the sex-ed thing was blown out of proportion... that Obama only wanted kids to learn about the dangers and warnings of sexual predators as part of a comprehensive sex education program aimed at older children. I guess we'll just have to agree to disagree. I'm certainly not going to waste time looking it up. I trust my friend and he'll only pass along emails that have been properly vetted and fact-checked.

Rest assured, those email chains are not hoaxes. Because the original sender has done his research (and usually the original sender is a Marine, or reformed Democrat, or a good Christian, or Andy Rooney). In fact, these days the email calls the liberals' bluff, daring them to call it a hoax. The message may start out by saying: "If you don't believe me, look it up on the Internet."

And sure enough, when someone does a Google search, the first 100 or so "finds" are based on the email chain that was originally sent, which had been picked up by all the conservative websites. So any research a liberal has to do to counteract our "truth" takes more time than he anticipated. Hell, by the time he can find enough info to refute three of an email's claims, we've already gotten 10 more messages. Liberals can never catch up, because we're always a few steps ahead. By the time he comes back to me with the sex-ed thing, I'm already riled up about Van Jones.

So in conclusion, Obama is a traitor to his country. No lapel = Go to hell.

CHAPTER 10
Obama plays the blame game,
and that's why everything is his fault.

Obama spent his whole first term blaming former president George W. Bush for all the problems in America. The Recession, the high unemployment, the wars, the debt, any time he stubbed his stupid toe. But after awhile, you can't play the blame game any more. You have to take some blame yourself. Just admit you're an awful human being that should be put down like a broken-legged horse.

Like if you burned my house down three years ago, destroying everything I own, and I'm still rebuilding from the wreckage, I shouldn't be allowed to blame you anymore. Because after awhile, that burned-down house is my responsibility. Not yours.

And if my hands were burned in the fire, so I'm unable to properly feed myself, drive a car, work on a computer, operate a phone, wipe my ass or use the remote, I can't blame you for it. See, blame has a statute of limitations. So Obama should just STFU. Because thanks to him, my company ended holiday bonuses this year.

Contrast the Obama "blame everyone else" philosophy to that of his predecessor, the man who goes by one initial. W didn't blame Clinton for anything. He didn't blame Bubba for the budget surplus, or the peace, or the prosperity. Nope, 2001 was a clean slate, a time for Bush to move the country forward without the shackles of what occurred in the 1990s. Because in looking ahead, it's best to forget the past so we never know if we repeat it. That's from History class.

Obama doesn't just blame people. He blames things too. Like when the House Leadership rightfully points out that Obama's "spending spree" is putting us in great debt, thin-skinned Obama gets all "BlameGame" on us, saying it was stuff like wars, tax cuts, the Medicare Prescription Drug Plan and the Recession that cause the debt to rise. Hello! That stuff happened a long time ago! It's been 11 years since the tax cuts passed! How can they be hurting our deficit today? Does he know how stupid he looks when he says stuff like this?

And it truly irks me that when Republicans call Obama out on all the bad stuff he does, and rightfully point out he's the cause of every bad thing that's happening right now, Obama just responds by casting blame ("Let's all try to find common ground and work this out.") instead of being a man and just accepting responsibility for all the horrors he's brought upon this nation. Because everything bad that's real or imagined, big or small, is Obama's fault. A statement like that truly is a sad state of affairs.

CHAPTER 11
Janet Jackson's Boob = Teen Pregnancy

In my life I've seen some shocking things on live TV. But I've narrowed down the most shocking things to these three. In ascending order of shock value they go:

3.) The time that city council man committed suicide by shooting himself in the face

2.) 9/11

1.) Janet Jackson's exposed boob at the Super Bowl

I base my level of shock value on this simple criteria: At what age would I let my kids watch this? The higher the age, the more shocking the item in question.

For the city council suicide, I'd say 13. Because it shows the dangers of firearms while also showing how politics work on a local level.

For 9/11, I would say 15 or 16, mainly because of the magnitude of the event. While much of what we learn (the bravery of firefighters, the heroism of Rudy Guliani and George W. Bush, the unadulterated evil of Muslims, especially the terrorist ones) is important for kids to know, the horrifying shock of that day is more than a child can absorb at one time. Plus they need a certain maturity to handle the images on screen.

But the Janet Jackson thing? I would never let them see it, no matter what the age. At least with the city council thing, there was some sort of reason for it. The man was under investigation or something, and felt he had no other way out. It's sad, but at least as a parent I can teach my kids a lesson and encourage them that a cry for help doesn't have to be answered with the barrel of a gun.

With 9/11, I can tell them no matter how convoluted and misdirected their motives ("The terrorists hate our freedoms."), I could at least tell my kids there was a reason, at least from the terrorists' point of view.

But Janet Jackson. It defies explanation. It was such an unexpected shock, on the night of one of America's most important events (Super Bowl Commercial Sunday).

To be perfectly honest, I didn't notice it that night. But the buzz was profound the next day at work. It was all anyone could talk about. To think that CBS allowed this to happen, to show a pixelated nipple from a distance on national TV... it was just overwhelming. I could barely work at all that day. At least I couldn't after 10am, when Betsy from Accounting brought it up.

And since I couldn't get any work done from the distraction, I quickly went on an online fact-finding mission, to find a picture of this nipple. Fortunately, I only had to search for a minute, when I saw a closeup of the nipple on the home page of the Drudge Report. I nearly screamed. CBS allowed THIS to be shown? How dare they? And thank God for courageous people like Matt Drudge, exposing and condemning CBS for the act of showing Janet Jackson's nipple, by showing Janet Jackson's nipple.

By the end of the day, it was apparent that while 1 billion people saw the Super Bowl, 5 billion people had by now seen Janet Jackson's nipple up close. The die had been cast. Could the nation come together to make it through this defining moment in time?

I didn't care. In that chaotic time it was every man for himself. I just cared about me and my family. Knowing that my kids could see the nipple online, I quickly canceled our Internet service. It disappointed my daughter, who was researching a report for school ("The Y2K Phenomenon") and who had to use grandma's old set of encyclopedias instead (let's just say she didn't get an A). And every year since then, I've kept my family from watching the Super Bowl. It's just too risky.

And if Janet Jackson's boob as seen on TV was this horrific for us, imagine what it did to poor Justin Timberlake, who saw it live and in person. Think of the toll it took on him, seeing a nipple for the first time in his life in front of all those people. Something that should have been so special and on his wedding night was suddenly thrust at him front and center in front of a billion people across the world. Obviously he hasn't been the same person since, throwing himself at every beautiful woman who comes along, playing in golf events, acting, singing, hosting MTV award shows... the poor guy is doing all he can to fill the void that came from his traumatic experience.

But JT aside, we must consider the ramifications on this nation... the fallout from Nipplegate. Now I don't have the statistics in front of me, but I'm convinced that every unwanted pregnancy, and every instance of pre-marital (and some horrible post-marital) sex is the direct result of seeing Janet Jackson's nipple. Now rest assured I've done my part to help. I've written my congressional representative, asking to consider a bill where the Jackson estate must pay child support for all teen pregnancies. I haven't gotten a direct response to my letter yet, which is really shredding my confidence in the democratic process. But I keep resending it, just in case.

And where is Obama for all this? Why hasn't he made a statement on the nipple? Sure it happened five years before he took office, but what does he have to lose by commenting on it?

Unless he's in favor of the nipple. Maybe he likes all nipples. Maybe he'll force us to expose our nipples for everyone! Nipples out, people! It makes sense. Why else would he hide behind the "No Comments" he's not making to the nipple questions that aren't being asked? Something big is at play here, and the more Obama doesn't talk about it, the more I suspect him of turning this country into Nippleville.

And I'm this close to having my nipples removed, just to show Obama up when that big Nipple Day comes. Then I can say to him, "In your face!" In fact, I may not even wait until then. I'll get the nipples removed this month, and then next time Obama's in town, I'll wait in the rope line for him to walk by, and instead of shaking his hand I'll lift my shirt and scream: "Remember Janet Jackson! My nipples are not for public viewing!" I bet that gets a reaction.

CHAPTER 12
Stimul-useless

Obama reminds me of a kid at a birthday party who insists he gets the biggest piece of cake every time, and that he gets his first. How else do you explain the way he rammed through the economic stimulus within weeks or months after taking office? He could've started with something less significant, like naming a post office after the president of Kenya. But NOOOO. He had to go and try to fix the economy and stave off a Great Depression.

Instead of going for a big and bold public works initiative that us conservatives would have objected to from the start, he went with a mix of tax cuts and road construction projects and infusions of money that us conservatives objected to from the start. So even when he tried to go big, he only went half-assed. It's not like he had a chance in hell of satisfying us conservatives anyway.

The stimulus itself was full of lies. For example, the tax cut. I don't remember getting a tax cut when that thing passed, do you? My paycheck was practically the same, except there was a little more money in it, which I thought was a glitch in the payroll department. So I ask you, where was the tax cut? When Bush cut taxes, you knew about it. We got a child tax credit (Boom! $500). That was free money! That's how it works... money in the hand is proof that we got what's coming to us. So the stimulus had nothing for me.

The stimulus itself was a failure. That is irrefutable fact. Like the timelessness of "Mama's Family."

How did it fail? Simple. Obama promised it would bring unemployment rate down to about 7 percent. But it only brought it down to 9 percent. FAIL. And don't blather on about how the Recession was actually worse than anyone imagined, or the OMB's report that the stimulus saved 2 million jobs, and that the unemployment rate would now be 11 percent without the stimulus. I still call it a failure, much like a C student who promises to get an A, but only gets a B. FAILURE.

Not only that, the stimulus cost $700 BILLION. That $700 billion put us $15 TRILLION in debt! And that pisses me off. Because the national debt, while a bit of a concern of mine before, has really riled me up these last couple years. Now my number one issue is to bring the debt down, without cutting taxes. Obama doesn't seem to get this simple logic. Nope, it's just spend, spend, spend and tax, tax, tax. Sure he hasn't raised taxes, *yet*. And sure government is technically smaller (if the number of government jobs and money spent in government is your standard of measurement) under Obama than it was under Bush, but I don't need these subjective benchmarks to disprove what I find is a fun sentence to say:

"Obama likes to spend like there's no tomorrow, and tax the rich like there's no today."

Obama is a tax & spend liberal. And no amount of facts will get me to change my opinion on that. You may have your facts. But I have my truth. My truth wins. And fits better on a bumper sticker.

Regardless, when it comes to addressing Obama's platform, I like the Republican gameplan (Stall). But it will take some sacrifice and teamwork on the part of the middle class. Meanwhile, what the Republicans have to do is keep Obama from passing any of his ludicrous proposals for "job creation". The leadership in the House (John Boehner and Eric Cantor, the Batman & Robin of Congress) can propose and even pass bills the Senate and president would never accept (scrapping

Medicare, dropping capital gains tax rates to negative 10%, giving Paul Ryan his very own Girls Gone Wild tour bus). This way NOTHING gets done. Gridlock rules! Then Republicans can say that Obama's policies which never really got enacted (except for the debacle stimulus and parts of Obamacare) failed. And by going one step further, Republicans can say this gridlock is proof that "government is broken". And since Republicans are all about small government, they can also say "Hey, we hate government, because it works so terribly. Just look at how it's 'working' right now. So vote for us as your government representatives."

In our role as concerned conservative citizens, we have to let government fail to do ANYTHING until Election Day. This way the blame for the do-nothing Congress can fall on Obama's shoulders (because people blame the president first), and we get the Republican candidate elected. Then we're free to pass all the things we want (more tax cuts, fewer regulations, no Obamacare, no minimum wage, no unions, higher and deadlier border fences, no birth control, no gay anything, internment camps for atheists, and so on.) And I'm sure that once the Republicans in power get all the economic-related stuff out of the way, they'll get to the moral issues (abortion) next. Just like they've promised us for the last 40 years.

But we have to do our part. That means a few more months of sacrifice. That means not buying things to spur the economy (which is easier for those of us whose savings have run out). That means working extra hard at your job, doing the work of two or three people so your boss doesn't feel obligated to hire anyone, thus keeping the unemployment rate up. It means that if you are unemployed, you hang in there! Cat food is an acquired taste, so stick with it! It means preventing your kids from doing their homework (or any schoolwork) and getting good grades, so we can show how our public schools have failed our kids. It means not bitching when the dirty air you breathe gives you cancer. Or the dirty water you drink gives you rabies. Or the meat you eat gives you E. coli. Or the bridge you drive on collapses just as your drive on it. Or the eggs you eat are laced with strychnine. And if you suspect terrorist activity, DON'T SAY ANYTHING! Another terrorist attack, which would have helped Bush even more in 2004, will be killer to Obama in 2012. And by warning the authorities, the terrorist attack you prevent today could prevent a Republican landslide on Election Day. Think about it.

So hang in there! It's not much longer until Election Day! Then things will change and we'll all be happy.

CHAPTER 13
Cutting down oak trees to spite ACORN

ACORN stole the election in 2008 for Obama. I'm not sure how they were able to manipulate the electoral process to such a degree, but we all know they did it. It's not like he could have won fair and square. Cheating is in his blood. He's from Chicago, and Chicago politics and politicians are corrupt. Ergo, he's corrupt.

Sure, the final election returns reflected what just about every pre-election poll was showing at the time, but that's the evil genius of ACORN. Obviously this non-profit organization, with loosely affiliated networks across the country, managed to manipulate the polling process for months beforehand while altering the landscape in voter registration to ensure only Democrats could register. Meanwhile they registered dead people to vote as Democrat, stuffed the ballot boxes on Election Day, rigged the ballots and electronic voting machines, sabotaged the vote-counting process and then paid everyone who worked at the news channels to "call it" for Obama, and then paid hush money to people who knew the truth, at least until Inauguration Day, when by then it was too late. Brilliant.

Something this powerful needed to be stopped. But who would have guessed they would have stopped themselves?

Fortunately it turns out that ACORN is also a prostitute ring, run by pimps. Who knew?

A man with a hidden camera went to ACORN office after ACORN office, posing as a pimp himself and asking if he could get some ho's. At least, that's how I remember the story. Now most offices told him to get lost (ACORN is nothing if not impolite), which showed them how far and widespread this hooker network truly was. Their silence only confirmed their guilt. Plus most ACORN offices have in-house pimps... they don't want out-of-network pimps they weren't sure they could trust.

But then, one office cracked and fell for the brilliant ruse. And through some crafty video editing, some well-timed indignation by radio hosts and Fox News guests, and ACORN's unbelievable denials, the group's reputation and existence was in doubt. Then a few politicians got mad, too, demanding the end of federal funds for ACORN. And knowing that Democrats had neither the time or a concise (6 words or less) argument to defend a group that had helped tens of thousands of people register to vote, Republicans knew they had a winner. See you later, ACORN. Don't let the pimp's stretch limo door hit you on the ass on the way out.

However, it was too late to change the result of the 2008 election. Which is truly a sad state for the greatest country on Earth. What do we tell our children when scattered and inconsistent anecdotal evidence is not enough to have a presidential election "do over"? Will they lose faith in the ideal of "America"?

But moving forward, we must use the lessons of ACORN as a teaching moment, and a way to further our conservative cause as we rid the world of Obama and his cronies. First, now that we've established ACORN as corrupt and inherently evil (and a by-product of liberal ideas to get more people, ahem black people, to vote), we can now discredit anyone or any cause that's even remotely associated with it.

Back when he was a community organizer, Obama knew a couple guys in ACORN. I'm sure he even helped them out. Hello! We've got a smoking gun in Obama's hands now (and not the good kind of smoking gun that you can take into a bar in Ohio). He's tainted by ACORN more than ever. Put the pieces together. He was instrumental in the rise of ACORN (no need to explain how... there'll be time for explanations later), the same group that stole the 2008 election for him. So Obama did something for them, and they did something *for him*. Yep, this is worse than Watergate. And the Holocaust.

And to think, ACORN may have gotten away with it if not for the heroism of James O'Keefe, his big hat, and his little camera.

And anyone associated with ACORN is screwed now. Obama nominates someone for judge... well he once had coffee at a Starbucks one block from an ACORN branch. See you later, "your honor". Obama names someone to a Cabinet subcommittee. But because that someone received an email blast from Move-on.org, which supports ACORN, she's gone. Have a nice life.

So even if ACORN is dead, we can still bring it to life, to kill the careers of Obama-lovers.

CHAPTER 14
That birth certificate doesn't mean shit.

I don't like the term "birther". It sounds condescending. I prefer the term "Afterbirth Team."

Because we're the ones concerned about where Obama was "after his birth." See, it makes sense. Like being called a Teabagger. Nothing wrong with that.

Now one look at Obama (and one look at his name) tells you that he isn't a "true" American. That's Exhibit A right there.

I know his team says he was born in Hawaii. How convenient is that? A state so far off the mainland, and one where their inhabitants don't look like you and me (except for Magnum PI). And the state has a funny-looking name, too. Just like Obama. But guess what? Obama doesn't even look Hawaiian. Seriously, he was grasping here. How long did he think this cover story would last?

So concerned citizens spoke up, demanding to see his birth certificate. Because we wanted to know where the hell he came from (and if it was a place that even HAS birth certificates, wink wink, Kenya). But Obama wouldn't play ball. In fact, he tried to throw us off the trail with copies of newspapers from when he was born, which had his birth announcement. He showed us a *copy* of his birth certificate. The governor of Hawaii confirmed he was born there. The hospital where he was born confirmed it. Which only proved one thing...

The lies just don't end with this guy! How far would he take a cover-up, and how far back in the past did this web of deception begin? Obviously Obama got his plan in motion before he was even born, so that he could infiltrate the newspaper, pretend to born in that hospital, and Photoshop childhood pictures of himself with Hawaiian items in the background. Items like volcanoes and the Pacific Ocean.

But even if you believe these lies, you can't deny the obvious: He has a funny name! And he's black but not really! All Obama has to go on are documents, notarized records, and testimony of witnesses. How flimsy.

So who blinked in this important battle? Obama blinked! He finally released his "real" birth certificate because the controversy was a "distraction." Yet another lie. I wasn't distracted. I liked complaining about the birth certificate. It was a great part of my day.

But wait! I didn't get to see that birth certificate in person. I didn't get to touch it. Or make sure Hawaii was spelled correctly. They didn't display it in the Smithsonian or next to the Constitution. Or take it cross-country like a bookmobile or Dave Matthews' tour bus. He just had a news conference, showed it to reporters, who confirmed its authenticity (liberal media, big surprise). Did Obama really think this would end the controversy? Does he know anything about us? We don't give up on anything! Even if we look ridiculous, we'll keep at it. That "South will rise again" stuff? Oh, it's happening. We ain't giving up on that, either.

Anyway, isn't it suspicious it took Obama so long to show the birth certificate? I guess the forger needed more time to get it right. Plus I, like so many other people and bloggers (bloggers, mainly), wanted to see the *long-form* birth certificate, whatever that is. Honestly, I never knew such a thing existed before the Obama scandal. Maybe it's something they use just for presidents. But now that I knew what it was, I wanted to see it, no matter how long that long form was. But it never came, as far as I know. And I bet a Google search will show me that what Obama did release is a fake, anyway. The fight continues!

What will satisfy us? What will prove to us that Obama was born in Hawaii? Simple. We need video evidence of the birth. And conception, too for that matter. With that day's local newspaper clearly visible in the shot. And a radio playing in the background that says the date, time and place. And the doctor announcing, "It's a boy! The future president of the United States, Barack Hussein Obama, born today in Hawaii (a real state) on August 4th 1961." The doctor must say these words verbatim, or the evidence is worthless.

Now I know what you're thinking. John McCain was technically born in Panama, but that's neither here nor there. I'm sure if he had won in 2008, the shoe would have been on the other foot. Liberals would have screamed and wailed and hooted and hollered and gotten all high on LSD and acid. And we conservatives would have let them do so, as is their Constitutional right. We would have given them the courtesy they never give us.

You may think this whole endeavor is unfair, since Obama was the first president to have his citizenship publicly questioned, along with his legitimacy to hold the office of president. And I say to that, "He has a funny name!" It's not just because he's black. Or because we're pissed off he won (stole) the 2008 election. It was all about the funny name. Our presidents aren't supposed to have funny names. (Except maybe Grover Cleveland). The office is too important. We need the rest of the world to respect us. That's why classic first names like George and William and James and John and

Richard work so well. They're strong sounding names. They don't elicit snickers or someone saying, "How do you spell that?"

Liberals may say that the strong-sounding names I mentioned are more likely to be "white" names. Well those liberals are playing the race card again.

See what I did there? I took an accusation of racism and turned it around. The easiest way to do that is to say, "You're playing the race card." Liberals are never sure how to respond to this. It's a confusing accusation to them. Because then they're scared they might be doing or saying something racist. And that scares the hell out of them. Because they all have that doubt that maybe, just maybe, they're a tiny bit racist. And what if their friends found out?

So claiming the race card is a good way to stop any discussion that involves race. "Was Johnny Mathis black?" You're playing the race card. "Inner city kids don't have access to a quality education because the budgets don't allow it." You're playing the race card. "I got the Ace of Spades." You're playing the race card. And if a liberal denies this ("I'm not playing the race card.") all you have to say is, "Yes you are. The more you deny it, the more racist you are." And when he says, "I'm not a racist," you just reply, "Sure, whatever you say. Though you really are denying it quite loudly. Which is what a racist would say."

CHAPTER 15
Everything is Destroying America.

Taxes. Abortion. Muslims. People who look like Muslims. People who look like people who look like Muslims. Atheists. Gays. Gay marriage. Gay drivers. Illegal aliens. Legal aliens. Steroids in baseball (but not football). Catholic schoolgirl uniforms. The kids today. Catcher in the Rye. Coke Zero. Medicinal marijuana. The HPV vaccine. AIDS. Unions (both private and public but especially public). Frivolous lawsuits. Legitimate lawsuits. Voter fraud. Rosie O'Donnell. The Simpsons. Liberal professors. Gun control. Indian casinos. Indiana casinos. Welfare (not corporate welfare, the welfare for "poor" people). Comedy Central. Hot lunch programs. Nuclear weapons in nations not named USA or Israel. Zooey Deschanel. Song lyrics with swear words. The idea that "The Hunger Games" can actually happen. The Miami Heat. An Inconvenient Truth. Not being able to ride a snowmobile in a state park. Two parents working. Augusta National Golf Club letting in women. Zombies. The Toyota Prius. Pawn Stars. The iPhone. Recycling. The kids today. The CW. Bill Clinton. Al Gore. Jimmy Carter. The corpse of FDR. Blu-ray®. Terrorists. Eco-terrorists. People who complain about school bullies. Parole. YouTube. Facebook. Twitter. AOL. Removing "Under God" from the Pledge of Allegiance. Higher fuel mileage standards. Those throwback uniforms the Packers wear once in a while. Harry Potter. MSNBC. CNBC. NBC. Glee. Hookers that don't look the way they do in the movies.

All these things, on their own, have the power to destroy America. Open a book, read a blog, check your email, watch Steve Doocey. It's a fact. America is loaded with things that, left unchecked, will destroy her. And this list grows day by day. See, orange golf balls just made the list. Just this second.

With so many things destroying America, it's a wonder America hasn't been destroyed already. How lucky are we that NONE of these things has caused our doom?

Or was it even luck at all? What saved us? It was conservatives. And maybe God, too. If not for us conservatives, America would be destroyed. So you're welcome. But I'm not asking for any credit. But the occasional free meal at Arby's would be nice. I'm at the one on Massillon Road in Uniontown, Ohio every Tuesdays and Thursdays at noon. Stop by, chat, and foot the bill.

You may ask how we've saved you, but that's a discussion for another time. Just know that you should always be afraid, and know that conservatives are your only hope. If liberals gain power, it will take about 10 seconds for something from that list (or maybe even something else!) to destroy America.

So play it safe. Vote for the conservative. Or be destroyed.

Postscript:

You may think destruction won't be so bad. Maybe it'll be painless, or so fast you won't even feel it. Or you think I'm just exaggerating what I mean by "destroy". As if I'm talking about some psychological destruction.

Nope. I mean literal, salt the earth, all things dead, Cormac McCarthy's "The Road" times a million destruction. And it won't be a quick, painless, nuclear-bomb-dropped-on-your-forehead death. Nope, it'll be slow, blood-curdling, weeks-long pain. A pain that's bad enough to have you scream your throat out, but not so bad you pass out from shock. It'll be like all those "Saw" movies. Only with a lot more saws. And for the liberals it'll be much worse, because then they'll wake up in Hell. So I guess it's not all bad.

CHAPTER 16
If we believe we're being oppressed, then it must be true

The older I get, the more I realize that "they" are keeping me "down". "They" are oppressing "me".

If not for "them", my true potential would be reached, I wouldn't be underpaid at work, I wouldn't have to pay taxes, and I would be married to Giselle Bundchen. And she wouldn't mind that Miranda Kerr is my girlfriend. So you can see why I'm quite angry at "them."

Who are "them"? It's hard to tell.

Listening to talk radio, it's the parasite liberals. Listening at church, it's the people who don't go to church. Or at least they don't go to *my* church. Listening to my congressman, it's unions and people on welfare and cops taking too much overtime and foreign nations taking too much of our money. Listening to my grandpa, it's the Beatles.

But I keep it simple. The "they" are those who voted for or ever had a non-threatening thought about Obama. They're the ones keeping me and those like me down. And by doing that, they are actively trying to destroy America. It's stunning to me that tens of millions of people can be actively involved in a plot to destroy this great country of ours while turning us against each other. But there you have it. I'm sure they have meetings and planning sessions and "love-ins" where they discuss how they'll destroy America this week.

In fact, I've asked some liberals point-blank why they want to destroy America. It's a fair question. And they look at me like *I'm* the crazy one. Some actually deny their destroy-America intentions by saying, "I want what's best for America. Why would I destroy a nation that I call home?" And they seem truly sincere, leading me to believe they're completely hypnotized, under some spell that will culminate when their skinny Emperor uses the Force to summon them into an all-out attack to destroy America. That's the saddest part. These people have no idea what is waiting for them. They have no idea of their forthcoming role as destroyers of this nation. They don't know how they are the key to our nation's destruction. And thus I find it more and more rational to murder them. It's a pre-emptive act of self-defense. It's either them of my family and country.

But I digress.

My first eye-opener into how oppressed I was came in church. Growing up I assumed all families went to church. And with a place of worship on most every corner, I figured there was literally a church for everyone.

So imagine my surprise to hear the pastor talk about "them". In the Bible, they were the people who hassled Jesus all the time, asking him about taxes and crucifying him. "They" hated Jesus because He was so awesome. Nobody was as badass as Jesus (don't worry, it's OK to swear when you're talking about Jesus). He had answers to everything ("Pay to Caesar what is Caesar's. Pay to the Lord what is God's." Boo-Yah!), he turned water into wine, and he made long hair and beards cool again. So it was hard to imagine ANYONE hating Jesus. But it was true. "They" hated Him. Haters were everywhere in the Bible.

And the "they" of today are just as bad as the "they" of back then. Essentially, if you're not a Christian, you're the equivalent to the haters and killers of Jesus. And you're oppressing me with your hateful agenda, the main part of it being that you don't see things my way. You may not think you have an agenda, but that's how the devil works. Just because you don't have a clipboard and a checklist of demands, that doesn't mean you don't have an agenda.

Each week in church, our pastor talks about "them." They're the ones who call us "Jesus freaks". I've never been called a Jesus freak, but I hope to someday. So based on this anecdotal evidence of name-calling, it's fair to say that "they" exist (no doubt about it) and are therefore doing the work of the devil. Just like the West Memphis Three.

How numerous are these oppressors? Let me drop some knowledge right in here: 20% of the population believes in evolution (morons!). So we got that contingent to go up against. We're the underdogs. Our 80% against their 20%. And we can't underestimate them. While 99% of our politicians, Supreme Court justices and presidents call themselves Christians, the oppressors stay strong. I'm not sure how they do it, but the best thing we can do is keep on talking about this threat every Sunday at church, every Sunday at Bible Study, and every day online. And tell our friends and neighbors and family. And post it to Facebook. Because the best way to stop a threat is to give it a lot of attention.

But it doesn't stop at the non-Christians. Listen to talk radio and you'll hear about all the "freeloaders" weighing our society down with their laziness, hand-outs and repeat trips to the sundae bar at Golden Corral (I know it's all you can eat, but you're taking all the Heath Bar chunks!). They don't seem to care that they oppress me by taking what is rightfully mine (my tax dollars).

And I know these freeloaders are taking what's mine, because the news I watch and read reminds me of it every day. And the more I hear it, the madder I get. And the madder I get, the more I need to hear about it. It's a vicious cycle that can't be broken. And with each cycle I feel more oppressed, and I can't be satisfied with the life I have. Even though I have a decent house, a bed to sleep in, I never go hungry and I have my health. "Nobah-dy knows, the trouble I've seen. Nobah-dy knows, but Jesus."

CHAPTER 17
I'm not a racist

You can't call me a racist.
Because I would have sex with Halle Berry.

I could end the chapter right there, confident that I've proven my point. But I believe in overkill.

It's fairly common to see liberals call out conservatives as "racists." And that's far from the truth. Sure, all racists may vote Republican, but not all Republicans are racists. Touché.

Now I'm not going to defend myself by saying that "some of my best friends are black." Because that's not the case. But some of my best friends *could* be black, if they weren't already born white. Hey, I can't determine who tries to be friends with me, OK? And black people haven't approached me and asked "Could we be friends?", so it's not my fault. Man up, black people! Give me some love, fo-shizzle!

So maybe I sometimes feel like black people don't always work as hard as white people. Or I don't like it when white people marry black people (especially the black man & white blonde woman combination). And then have kids. And I get uncomfortable when I walk down a street at night and wonder if any black people are lurking. And I think Obama is a big stupid poopy pants (notice I didn't say "black" in describing him. A racist would.). And I think that black people are inferior to white people. Now does that really make me a racist? Maybe a bit bigoted. Or prejudiced. But racist? No way!

I don't go out wearing a white sheet, burning crosses on front yards or lynching people. That's what a racist would do. Me? I'm just a purebred guy that's proud of my white heritage, and who prefers the company of white people over any other race and would like it if black people went back to Africa. Is that so wrong?

Besides, I stand by my Halle Berry argument. And I will kick it up a notch to include:

Rihanna. Beyonce. Angela Bassett. Sanna Lathan. Zoe Zaldana. Thandie Newton. That black girl that was on Friends. No, the other one. And lots more I can't name, like the woman in the Victoria's Secret catalogue, that one woman who was on the Amazing Race. That cheerleader they panned to during a Broncos game last year. And Lena Horne when she was young.

CHAPTER 18
Defunding Planned Parenthood and NPR will create jobs. Here's how.

It's simple, really. Any jobs creation program requires spending cuts, because creating jobs ain't free, and how else are we going to get more money to pay for that job creation? With taxes? As if.

So the logical solution is to cut budgets on the stuff that people don't really need. NPR and Planned Parenthood for starters.

Now I don't listen to NPR, because I like *interesting* news, not 10 minutes on the inventor of the ukulele. And I don't really know what Planned Parenthood does (besides murder crying babies that would grow up to be Miss America and President and the world's leading thoracic surgeon).

But one thing Planned Parenthood and NPR does do is piss me off, so I like the idea of defunding them. Plus defunding them pisses off the liberals, which makes me happy.

And by cutting their funding which comes from our tax dollars, we have more money in the budget for a REAL jobs program. A program that includes rolling back expensive and restrictive regulations on business (Oh, your warehouse needs proper ventilation? Cry me a river... of sludge) and giving tax cuts to business owners. And those owners will use that money to hire people. Because they like hiring people. It's fun for them! They love doing it. I know this is true because so many times I've asked for a job, and the owner always says, "I wish I could hire you, but I can't." See, it's one of his wishes! But the big bad government is keeping his wishes from coming true. It's like they put a cork on the lamp he's rubbing. (Oh wait, that's not a lamp. It's his secretary's ass.)

And would we miss NPR? Sheesh, I've gone my whole life without it. You don't need it to live. It's not like air or water or beer. Plus they get tons of money from "listeners like you" and Alec Baldwin. Why do they need *my* tax dollars when the people who actually listen to it can pay for it themselves? Why subsidize something no one cares about, when we can use that money to subsidize something everyone uses? Not NPR. How about O-I-L.

You may say I'm just trying to get rid of NPR because of its liberal bias. That is wrong. If a conservative radio station got tax dollars, I would want them off the air. Scout's Honor.

Oh, you say NPR doesn't have a liberal bias? Have you heard NPR? Really, have you? I'm asking, because I haven't. But from what I understand, they're all about giving facts, littering the airwaves with sourced information, and avoiding speculation. They don't reflexively shower a Republican politician or idea with praise. They don't even yell at each other. And as I said before, facts just don't do it for me. "Facts" are what you find in a liberal's argumentative toolbox. A conservative comes armed with passion and volume, which can drown out facts any time. Here's an example:

"In 1492, Christopher Columbus commissioned the king and queen of Spain to…"

"NPR IS ANOTHER EXAMPLE OF SOCIALISM RUN AMOK UNDER AN OBAMA PRESIDENCY!"

See? Which argument stood out? I rest my case. And NPR should rest in a casket.

Now on to Planned Parenthood. It's neither planned, nor is it about parenthood. The pregnancies it aborts are "unplanned". And when they do their abortions, suddenly there is no "parenthood." It's all about planning… to not be a parent!

Now Planned Parenthood will tell you they do more than abortions. Whatever, those breast cancer screenings are just a front. Like when the mob opens a Laundromat, but you know in the back room the mobsters are all racketeering. And stuff.

All that other stuff Planned Parenthood does is just a way to "upsell" to an abortion. It's like going to McDonald's. "Would you like an abortion with that?" They got doctors in the back just chomping at the bit to abort babies. And our tax dollars fund this!

So if we defund Planned Parenthood, women won't be able to get abortions anymore. Or at the least, we'll make it a little more dangerous, and that will have them thinking twice about A.) getting an abortion and B.) getting themselves pregnant in the first place.

Now people may complain if, by making abortions more difficult to get (or against the law), that women desperate for an abortion will risk their lives by getting one from an incompetent doctor, and they might die. Let me address the elephant in the room: That may be OK, in the long run.

Hear me out. Often the truly great men are the ones who deliver the hard truths. Like when Thomas Edison said, "Ma'am, you're going to be blind forever."

So imagine if abortion is illegal. First off, it would be much tougher to find an abortion doctor. A Google search can only get you so far. So making the search difficult can just exasperate our abortion-seeker. And since she's pregnant, she'll get tired more quickly too. And just give up the quest. And a few months later she gives birth to the light of her life and we can all leave her alone. All alone. Because we would have given her all the help she needs.

But some will get lucky and find an abortion doctor. That can't be helped. Some people are more resourceful than others. But that resourcefulness might be their undoing. Because they may fall victim to an unsafe abortion and die. That just tears my heart out. But there's no getting around the occasional tragedy. But that tragedy can actually be a silver lining. Which is why we make that tragedy news, to get the word out to other abortion-seekers, who know that an abortion equals death all right... to them. And then no one else will ever be so desperate to take the risk in seeking an abortion. Ever. Problem solved.

And it all starts with defunding Planned Parenthood.

CHAPTER 19
A waterboard a day keeps the terrorists away.

I took a shower today, and some of the water ran down my face. Did I call the ACLU?

So what's the problem? To me, waterboarding sounds like a refreshingly good time, like something you might get at a day spa. First they put a moist rag over your face (like getting a shave at the barber), and pour some water over it. That's it! All that's missing is the cucumbers over the eyes! It's not torture. It's a day out with Samantha Jones!

I'm amazed waterboarding actually works on those Muslim terrorists. You'd think being out in the desert would make them thirsty, and they would love a refreshing drink! But they don't have the resolve of Americans. Because we're all like

Jack Bauer. Hook us up to a generator and send a few kilowatts through our genitals and we won't talk. Just name, rank and serial number. Then we'll spit in your face. We may yell in pain a bit, but we won't break. Keep punching us in the face (while somehow avoiding knocking out any of our front teeth) and we'll bruise up some, get a few cool scars, some cuts right above the eye, but we'll never talk.

So while we true Americans can handle damn near anything, the pacifists claim that handing a terrorist a drink of water amounts to "torture". Whatever.

If it is torture, then it's torture that works, by the way. It's how all those terrorist acts that were supposed to happen, never actually happened. Chances are while we sit here right now, a plot to blow up Mount Rushmore is being discovered and thwarted by "torture". Or at least, it should be. I like Mount Rushmore, and plan on chiseling Ronald Reagan's face up there one day.

Meanwhile, Americans can't be broken, ever. Torture doesn't work on us (the non-liberals anyway), but it does the job fine and dandy on the bad guys. So why is Obama so stupid as to let torture be called "illegal"? If anything, it's the greatest weapon we have in the War on Terror! We need more torture! Every day and every way! Bring out the rack! Why can't Obama see that?

Maybe because he's not one of those strong Americans like Jack Bauer. Maybe he's soft. Like if you do that "pretend to punch him" move, he'll probably flinch. And we don't need a president like that. That's why all candidates for president should have to submit to the "two for flinching" test, administered by Evander Holyfield. If you flinch, you're out. Reagan never would have flinched. And Rick Perry would just use his steely gaze to make you cry. (But a blind person would always pass the test, so we better watch out there. We don't want a blind person with access to "the button". He may mistakenly press it when he meant to change the channel.)

So this War on Terror could end tomorrow if we just legalize torture. But the Stupid Poopy Pants in Chief   won't do it. And that really hurts. More than I can bear.

CHAPTER 20
I'm not being offensive.
I'm just being funny.

If I say Michelle Obama looks like Chewbacca, or call Bill Clinton a child molester rapist, I'm just joking around. I don't really mean it! Sheesh, can't these libtards take a joke? They're like a bunch of Jew-killing Nazis.

See, when conservatives mock Michael J Fox, flailing their arms about and waving them like they just don't care, it's all in good fun. Because Parkinson's Disease is funny. Can't you see that? Perhaps it's a more sophisticated humor than what you're used to. In fact, when Rush Limbaugh went into his spastic gyrations, he wasn't making fun of Michael J. Fox. I believe it was an homage to him. Like a shout-out, a show of respect. It was Rush's way of saying, "I'm with you, brother. I can convulse just like you. Word is bond."

But if that wasn't a show of respect, then it was certainly a bit of harmless joking around. Like when you stuff a nerd in a locker and leave him there over the weekend. No one gets hurt. But for some reason, a group of people makes it their business to be offended.

So here's my advice for those liberals: when in doubt, assume it's a joke. I'm sure that if it sounds too ridiculous to be true, or so offensive that it nearly causes a brain aneurism, then it was merely the comic styling of a conservative commentator. If you don't find it funny, you obviously have no sense of humor.

Like when Herman Cain last year proposed a 20-foot high electrified fence to keep out illegals. By killing them. Of course he was joking! An 18-foot high fence would have been sufficient. But the liberals got all angry about it, like he was being serious. I'm glad Herman set the record straight by saying, "America needed to get a sense of humor." Hear hear. Because charring Mexican children is fuh-nee.

And that same time, Mike Huckabee told Ohio voters in favor of Issue 2 in last November's election that they should keep opponents of the referendum away from the polls by "letting the air out of their tires." Just jokes, people! Sure, maybe some who listened took Huck seriously and slashed some liberal's tires. I say, "Good for them! Joke's on you, liberals!"

Some liberals may contend that these jokes just aren't funny. Well, humor isn't always universal. You may laugh at "Modern Family". I laugh at "Modern Warfare". But please, don't try and tell me that these jokes are just subterfuges to reach the most extreme in our party with words they truly believe in. Because that... is really funny.

Joking is part of politics. It helps keep things light. And as we all know, humor is a defense mechanism. Against bad PR.

CHAPTER 21
The Death Penalty: An eye for an eye, and a lethal injection for a gram of crack

Former Los Angeles police chief Darryl Gates once said that "Casual drug users should be shot." And leftists found this to be controversial, and objected. Typical.

As usual, they took the quote out of context. Gates didn't say drug users should be shot "and killed." Just shot. Like maybe a bullet to the spine to cause a lifetime of paralysis. Or maybe a shot to the knee, where it really hurts. Or a gut shot like Mr. Orange got on "Reservoir Dogs," which, by the way, was a movie with no reservoir and no dogs. Tarantino a genius? I think not.

But Gates' quote provides a nice segue for me to talk about an emotionally charged issue: the death penalty. My stance, and this may surprise you: I'm all for it, and we don't use it enough. I'm not a big fan of lethal injection. I used to favor the firing squad. But using bullets to do it... seems like a waste of bullets. Maybe we should go with knives. Or spears. We can use them again and again.

As long as people are afraid of dying, the death penalty makes for a good deterrent. It's like how we punish our children. If they do something bad, we take away something important to them. Like their GI Joes. And when adults who are too old to play with toys anymore (Xbox games don't count as toys) do something bad, we take away something else, like their freedom. Or if they're really bad, their lives.

Now what makes a crime "really bad"? I think murder is on the list. You kill a person, you lose your "right to live card." Drug dealers? I say so, since drugs kill. So technically that's murder of a certain type. Drug addiction? I'd say so too, since all drugs can kill, even with one use. You never know when that one drag of marijuana is the one that causes you to go crazy and murder and eat your family. How about the occasional drug user? That's a toughie. But my gut says execute those people too. Because they're slowly killing *themselves*. And a lethal injection is so much more merciful than an overdose of drugs.

Other crimes like kidnapping are on the list. Because even if a kidnapper doesn't kill their victim, they've killed a part of their soul. Shoplifters? Maybe. What'd they steal? A pack of gum... jail time is good enough. A case of beer? Well, that's just a gateway crime. Next thing you know, they're hijacking beer trucks. So we better nip that shoplifter in the bud. That'd be wiser.

Of course liberals clutch their pearls at the idea of the death penalty. They say if we kill as punishment, we're no better than the criminals. Oh yeah? I'm a lot better than them... I have fewer tattoos, and I never killed anyone who didn't kill someone else (or commit a heinous crime). So we're not the same.

Liberals also whine that on occasion we execute an innocent person. Pish-posh! Our justice system is based on the idea that the accused is "innocent until proven guilty." PROVEN. That's how it's always worked. I defy you to give me an example of when it didn't.

And if by chance you find someone who may, maybe, could have been executed and not been guilty (which is like telling all our cops, lawyers and judges that they suck), I bet that same person committed some other crime and had it coming. The cop-killer who didn't kill that cop? He probably stole a car once.

So the death penalty keeps people from running with the wrong crowd. Folks like me make blanket statements about running with the wrong crowd all the time ("The kids on that block are all criminals."). And by doing so, we're doing a service to them. We're encouraging them to pull themselves up by their bootstraps and make something better of their lives. Otherwise they may be falsely accused of a crime they didn't commit, just because they run with the wrong crowd. Our prejudices may therefore keep them away from the scene of the crime. And keep them out of jail. Or out of the knife throwing line.

CHAPTER 22
"He drinks the blood of babies"
Disturbingly true facts about Obama

- You'll get Hepatitis C if you share an elevator with Obama.
- He likes "Return of the Jedi" more than "Empire Strikes Back".
- He's a racist.
- He kidnapped the Lindbergh Baby.
- He poured the drinks at the Jim Jones colony.
- He blacklisted Macauley Culkin. Now he can't get a job anywhere.
- He was born in Kenya.
- To rebuild his energy, he drinks the blood of babies after his workouts. Because he's wary of Gatorade and its high fructose corn syrup.
- He's responsible for those Olive Garden commercials.
- He's a liberal.
- He was the most liberal senator ever. (Even more liberal than Bernie Sanders and Al Franken? I guess so.)

- He forces Sasha and Malia to do shots of Jagermeister every night before bed.
- He never learned to read Swahili.
- He once wore a brown belt and black shoes... at the same time.
- He opens some of his gifts on Christmas Eve.
- He can't pee if someone is at the urinal next to him.
- He can't bowl worth shit.
- He takes the elevator even if it's only two floors.
- He had sex with Michelle Obama.
- He doesn't know all three verses to The National Anthem.
- He's a Socialist.
- He's a Communist.
- He's in bed with Wall Street.
- He's a Muslim who went to a Christian church for 20 years.
- He never tips above 15%.
- He can't do the jitterbug.
- His abs aren't as defined as they could be.
- He won a Grammy, just like Milli Vanilli.
- He used to make his T's look like F's and his F's look like T's on his True/False tests in elementary school.
- He has a fake diary that he leaks to the press, and keeps his real diary hidden somewhere.
- He didn't drink a beer until he was 19.
- That smile... braces!
- One of the communities he organized still doesn't have an Arby's.
- He never gives Michelle flowers just to be nice.
- He totally screws up the "Shout!" dance.
- He wrote the script for "Gigli". And "Troll 2".
- He poops.
- And it smells.
- He's the reason the Buffalo Bills can't win the Super Bowl.
- He likes "St Elmo's Fire" better than "The Breakfast Club."
- He wears his jeans twice before having them washed, just throwing them over a chair by the desk rather than putting them in a hamper.

CHAPTER 23
The Federal Reserve.
Not really sure what they do.

From what I gather, the Federal Reserve, or the Fed, handles monetary policy in the United States. They raise and lower interest rates to ward off inflation and to keep the economy from cratering into a deep depression. They also have the power to print as much money as they want (or at least create an environment of monetary policy that allows the Treasury to print money. I learned that fact when I accidentally read a column by Paul Krugman. Guess what, he's NOT the guy from "Quincy".). I used to think printing money was a good thing. But it turns out that printing MORE money makes money worth LESS. Ironic, doncha think?

The Fed is owned by Ben Bernake, who seemed like smart enough guy when George W. Bush appointed him. But now he seems like a real dumb-dumb working for Obama. Maybe just being around Obama makes one dumber. Obama is human marijuana. Stand too close and you get stupid.

As much as they handle money, I don't think the Fed is a bank. But bankers blame them for a lot of stuff. Like when I apply for a loan and the banker tells me, "The rates went up today, just minutes before you applied for this loan. Don't blame me. Blame the FED." Thanks a lot, Bernake. I just wanted to buy an El Camino.

CHAPTER 24
Civil Rights. Not so Civil.

I'm not old enough to remember the Civil Rights movement. But from the archival footage I've seen, it seems it was all about protests and police cracking skulls and fights in the streets. What's so civil about that?

We could've had a lot less violence and a lot more peace if these Civil Rights movements never happened. Just ask Trent Lott (Never forget Trent!).

Now it seems the term "Civil Rights" has been shanghaied by other "groups" looking for "rights." Groups like women, the gays, and poor people (The so called 51%, 7% and 99% respectively). But this fight for equal rights is not worth the trouble.

History lesson: The reason for discrimination is because a certain group of people is unliked, or they make a bigger group uncomfortable. Guess what: getting equal rights, or the right to vote, or equal pay, or the right to marry who you want isn't going to change the fact that people don't like you. In fact, they may like you *less* as a result (and nothing is more important than being liked). So was it worth it? Was it worth all the markers and paint to make those signs, getting pepper sprayed, getting the fire hoses turned on you, getting your shoes dirty marching around? Of course not. You may have gotten a couple things: the right to vote, which almost half of us use in a presidential election, or the right to marry who you want (and if you watch enough "Married... with Children" you know that isn't so great). You may earn more money, but the company will just make you work harder for it, and you'll have to pay more taxes.

So to recap: you put your life at risk to earn rights that aren't so great in the first place, all while never changing the way people see you. My advice: just do your job, be content with what you have, and know that it's a lot better than being in Russia, where they judge people all the time.

CHAPTER 25
Education Fail:
Why don't they tell our kids Obama is a big stupid poopy pants?

I don't want my tax dollars spent on "frills" like education. Not when I have a simple way to fix education in this country. The quality of learning won't diminish, and the cost will decrease dramatically. It goes like this:

LET THE KIDS TEACH.

I know what you're thinking. Yep, it *is* brilliant.

It's so simple, I'm not sure why no one else has thought it up. But it takes a shrewd mind to come up with such solutions, a mind that hasn't been corrupted by the media, scientists, parents, schools, universities or Snapple caps.

Here's how it breaks down. A first grader can teach kindergarten. Second graders can teach first graders, and so on. *Because all you need to know to teach kindergarten is what a first grader knows!* You don't need to know algebra or how a bill becomes a law. Hell, if you can read "The Cat in the Hat" and add numbers up to 10, you qualify. Congratulations, Aiden. You're a teacher! Now stop peeing your pants.

Since we'll have kids doing the teaching, we won't have a use for unions anymore, and think of the money we would save. First, most people have no idea what a union is until they reach adulthood. So we won't even bring the notion up to these kids we got teaching.

"What a union?"

"Um... they're the guys who won the Civil War. Now get back to work. These kids aren't going to teach themselves!"

Next, we can keep their salaries nice and low. I bet you could get away with paying a nine-year old second grade teacher $20 a week. They're probably in awe when their Dad pulls a $20 bill out of his wallet, so imagine the joy and jubilation our kid has when we give him one of those EVERY WEEK.

Third, we won't have to pay any of their health insurance, because they would already be on their parents' plan. Score!

And fourth, we don't have to help pay their retirement either, because each kid may at most teach a year or two. Once they teach for a bit, they'll go back to school and learn how to get a real job.

Now there is some sort of crazy notion that education is a "right." That all kids should get one. WRONG! The fact we let all kids have access to education means they don't work at it. The kids today are lazy, they're undisciplined, and stupid. The reason for that is because they don't have any skin in the game. Since they KNOW they'll get an education for free, they don't work at it.

Seriously, what does a high school student have to inspire him to learn? If you give him a car, he won't take care of it. If he *earns* that car, he'll treat it like a newborn baby. So we have to make education worth paying for.

What, you think that getting into a good college, or graduating to get a decent job, is enough to get him to show up? NO! We need to charge his parents (and him) money to attend! (This could weed out the "undesirables"). We must punish him when he fails. And make him feel embarrassed.

That's why we need to let teachers beat and humiliate kids in any way they see fit. Just like the old days. When schools were awesome and all the kids behaved and were in 4H and Boy Scouts and ducked & covered.

If a kid gets out of line (or if a teacher thinks he's getting out of line, or if a teacher just doesn't like him), that teacher should be able to discipline the child... by any means necessary. I'm not saying we cut off the kid's thumbs (not on a first offense), but we can't go easy on him either. If the kid talks back, wash his mouth out with soap. With those granules found in the school's bathroom. If the kid falls asleep, crash a couple cymbals over his head. Or dump ice down his shirt. If a kid flunks a test, put him in The Hole. For a school day. Or a week. Or semester.

Oh, I didn't mention The Hole? This is great. It's based off Shawshank Redemption (the book, not the movie). On the first day of school, each kid is given a shovel, and during the course of that school day, they dig their hole somewhere on the school grounds. The faster they work, the better it is for them.

Because that hole they dig... is their hole. So they want it deeper and wider.

Then when they get sent to The Hole, they go to theirs, step inside, and an iron-bar door is closed and locked above them. It's not a solid door. That would be cruel. This way the sunlight can beam in, along with the rain and snow and rats.

I would also require all schools to recite the Pledge of Allegiance... before every class period. In fact, I think the phrase "under God" should be used in each line of the Pledge. "I pledge allegiance, under God,
to the flag, under God
of the United States of America, under God."

You get the idea. We want to make sure God hears us, and saving the "under God" for nearly the end means that He may miss it. God may duck out early because He has lots of stuff to do. Or maybe the kids aren't saying the Pledge with enough *feeling*. And God just decides to tune the ungrateful kids out. You just never know.

But the Pledge isn't enough. It's more of a warm-up act... where first the kids show their commitment to country. Then we must have them pray, to show their commitment to God. Seriously, I'm not sure why this is even debatable. It's like MC Hammer once said, "We got to pray just to make it today." (It sounds much better on cassette than in print.)

But liberals cry foul, calling out the idea that "Separation of Church and State" makes prayer in school unconstitutional. What liberals don't get is that SOC&S just means that churches don't have to pay taxes! That's what separates them. *Churches* don't have to pay taxes to the *state*. A school is not a state. It's a SCHOOL. If prayer in school was unconstitutional, it would be called "Separation of Church and School." But it's not. So pray away, kids! (As long as you're Christian. Muslims, leave the prayer mat at home.) Because the government can't stop you. And if anyone tries to stop you, we'll find a group of angry parents to give your principal hell and threaten to vote against the levy (which we would have done anyway).

Now I want to talk a bit about teacher unions. Yep, they're destroying America. For some reason, teachers think they don't have to pay as much toward their health care, or as much to their retirement, as the rest of us! I work in the private sector, and our management has put more of the responsibility and cost for retirement and health care in *our* hands (That's what freedom is all about). So the price of that freedom is for us workers pay a lot more when we get sick, or if we want to retire. Meanwhile, schools (which only exist thanks to my tax dollars) haven't tightened their belts at the same rate. And that makes me mad! It's not fair that teachers, based upon a contract (some would call it an unbreakable promise) feel they deserve what the rest of us don't have.

And where do those union dues go? To Democrats! That's right. It's not exaggerating to say that 130% of union dues go toward political contributions for Barack Obama and his cronies. That's sickening, especially since not all union members are Democrats. It would be like a bank using its profits (generated by customers) to lobby one party in Congress!

Besides, the union only exists to keep bad teachers (and good, experienced teachers who just cost too damn much) from getting fired. Now what is a bad teacher? Simple: one that gives my kid bad grades. My kid is a super-genius! He learned to read on his own at the age of 7! And if the teacher can't turn him into the class valedictorian, it's the teacher's fault. Bad teacher!

Once you become a teacher, you got it made. Summers off, sick time, days that end at 3pm, snow days, spring break. According to my calculations, teachers work six days a year. Plus the job is EASY. You just repeat what's written in the textbook, grade tests with the help of an answer key, and play Angry Birds when the kids take a quiz. And that's how it is until you retire at age 35 with a golden parachute of a retirement plan. Sign me up! Seriously, why didn't I get into this career?

And you just can't be fired. It's impossible! Just as long as you get tenure after five years. And as long as you continue your own education. And by the way, us taxpayers foot the bill for that continuing education. Because my tax dollars pay the teacher's salary, and that salary is used to pay for the teacher's continuing education. So you're welcome, teachers!

It needs to be easy to fire teachers. Because if you ask me, most of them are awful. Not the teachers I had. Most of them were great. But I'm the exception... the one fortunate person who had good teachers his whole school career. Lucky break for me.

But since most teachers suck, we need to fire them. Sure, a few great, experienced, irreplaceable teachers might get the axe because budget cuts require more salaries be slashed, but it's a small price to pay to get rid of the bad teachers. And by paying teachers less, we'll get much better teachers. Because we'll only get the ones who love teaching and who don't do it for money. They're the ones in it for the thrill of teaching. Lots of people like that are around, I'm sure.

Oh, and no more raises for teachers until THEY EARN IT. And how do we determine what makes a teacher deserving of such a raise? Simple. For every student of yours that goes on to become President of the US (as a Republican), or a billionaire, or inventor of something that changes the world as much as the personal computer or automobile did, then you get a one-time $100 bonus. Sounds fair to me. Because the best way to judge a teacher is on the greatness of the student. When that student becomes an adult. Oh, and if a student goes on to achieve greatness after the teacher has died, that money goes to the student.

But since we're replacing all the teachers with kids anyway, who gives a shit?

POSTSCRIPT
Now I wrote a lot about the schools, and as conservatives it's a lot to communicate to our liberal moron friends. As I've often stated, our arguments need to be quick, to the point, and totally flummox our opponent. The best way to do that is to deliver a simple solution to a big problem.

In the case of schools, all you need to say is, "We wouldn't have these problems if we still had prayer in public schools." In fact, this statement goes beyond just problems in education.

There's a build-up of nukes in the Middle East? "We wouldn't have these problems if we still had prayer in public schools."

There's a flu pandemic? "We wouldn't have these problems if we still had prayer in public schools."

You're impotent? "We wouldn't have these problems if we still had prayer in public schools."

It'll be a 6-minute wait on your McNuggets? "We wouldn't have these problems if we still had prayer in public schools."

Works every time. Try it today!

CHAPTER 26
Liberals "Protest." Conservatives "Rally."

I hate flannel.

No, strike that. I hate flannel when it's worn by East Coast liberals who are looking to make some sort of "fashion statement." Flannel is for farmers, and hunters. Not for some college boy who got a full ride to the University of Hooking Up and Getting Drunk on Daddy's Dime.

And then these candy-asses have the gall to wear flannel at their protests. But really, their protests are just an excuse to get high, screw around, and litter. It's what happened at all those Occupy protests, and it's what happened at Obama's Inauguration. Those liberals left a mess.

Meanwhile, conservatives and Tea Partiers rally for the cause without making a big ol' pigsty. And here's the proof:

One million people were at Obama's Inauguration. And it took a week to clean up all the garbage his liberal sheep left behind. I'd ask if they were raised in a barn, but we all know that's not the case. They were raised in Daddy's big mansion. But since they had a maid to pick up after them, they never learned how to clean up.

Meanwhile, one million people were at Glenn Beck's Restoring Honor rally in 2010. Of course, liberals say this number is inflated (like their egos! HA!). They say the real tally was about 87,000 (if you want to believe the jokers at CBS news. Check your font, Dan Rather!). But let me digress a bit to show you how conservatives arrive at their numbers. It's a process that doesn't require "counting" or "estimates" or "common sense".

First off, Glenn Beck himself combed the news and blog reports (and comments sections) all across the world wide web until he found a number he felt was reliably accurate. In his eyes. And that number was 300,000 to 500,000. (I know, it's not quite a million yet. But this is part of the process.). After that it's time for people like me to go into action. By people like me, I mean those who share my opinion, but who are also more famous than I am, so they get to be on TV. So someone like Michelle Malkin goes on TV and/or blogs, and cites Beck's number. Then she slyly pumps it up a bit more, just by doing a little "rounding up". No one gets hurt, and they're practically the same number. She'll say, "And reports say that up to 400,000 to 600,000 people showed up." *[Note the phrase "up to". These two little words and four little letters mean you can say damn near anything, whether it's reporting the number of people at a rally to communicating savings on a Ford Focus.]* During the course of the same interview, she then rounds up again, based on the number she just cited seconds ago. "So that means 5, 6, even 700,000 people were there. It was amazing. And Japanese internment camps were awesome! I can say that because I'm of Asian descent!"

Cue Drudge. He takes Malkin's number and makes it his headline of the day, with a slight, imperceptible modification: "1,000,000 at the Rally?" And there you have it. We have a million.

Liberals may sarcastically wonder why we don't just keep rounding up until we reach 5 million or 10 million of 250 million. To them I say we conservatives don't exaggerate (beyond what we conservatives would believe). We just provide the numbers that the liberal media is too afraid to reveal. Besides, ask anyone at the Restoring Honor Rally to say how many people were there, and they'll tell you it was a million. I know. I was there. And here is how the conversations generally went:

Me: What a crowd? I hear there's a million people here. What do you think?

Someone else: A million? I guess I can't argue with that.

Or how about this exchange:

Me: A million people are here. Mission Accomplished for Glenn Beck. He did it!

Them: Really?

Me: Really.

Them: *Really?*

Me: Really, really.

Them: Wow.

So that's the proof that one million people were at Glenn Beck's rally, the same number that was at Obama's inauguration. This provides us an apples-to-apples comparison of the liberal protestors to the conservative patriots.

Like I said, inauguration attendees left a ton of garbage. Glenn Beck's rally did not. Fact: Conservatives are clean. Liberals are trash-heads.

However, liberals also claim that maybe Glenn Beck's march was cleaner because only 100,000 people were there. (Fewer people = less littering. Cue the eye-rolling on my part). And they point out that no reputable source has claimed a million people were there. Oh really. What do you call the aforementioned Michelle Malkan and Matty Drudge? What do you call my neighbor, who was also there, and who said it "really seemed like a million people." Are you calling them liars?

Speaking of liars, let's talk a bit about the Occupy movement. Just kill these protestors (many of whom are college students with nothing to do, unlike the elderly in the Tea Party who have sacrificed the precious time they would normally spend seeking ways to fill their chasm of a void), and we have a lot less competition in the job force. Plus it's the only chance we'll get so many worthless liberals in the same place at the same time. When you get an opportunity like that, take it. Like if you could get in a time machine and kill thousands of Hitlers all at once, you would do it, right?

Now when I say "kill", I don't mean murder in cold blood. The blood can be any temperature for all I care. The cops can make these murders look like an accident. But they better be careful, since the lamestream media will report on this in such a way that it doesn't make those cops look like heroes.

Now when it comes to rallies and protests, what you see on TV may not be enough to tell if it's a conservative rally (good) or a liberal protest (bad). Here's a helpful guide to tell one from the other:

• Liberals shriek at their protests. Conservatives make higher-volume calls for change at their rallies. And carry guns.

• Liberals are angry mobs. Conservatives are groups of highly-charged concerned citizens gathered together.

• Liberals let their "freak flag" fly. Conservatives wave the flag of America.

• Liberals are Nazis. Conservatives are just walking in lockstep unison with one another in an effort to exterminate anyone who doesn't share their belief structure.

• Liberals don't wear red, white or blue. Conservatives wear nothing but.

• Liberals inhale pot smoke. Conservatives inhale oxygen from a portable tank.

There you have it. I'll see you at a rally where we object to a liberal protest.

CHAPTER 27
Kill people. Not jobs.

I make $32,000 per year, and I will defend to my last breath those who make $32,000 per hour. I know it doesn't make much sense, but I'm so far down this road, what the hell am I supposed to do? Besides, it's the job creators making

$32,000/hour that give me this $32,000/year job. And if we suddenly force them to make $31,900/hour, they'll get pretty pissed, won't they? And they'll take it out on me, by ensuring I make $0/year instead. So I must love and honor and cherish and worship the rich, while also fearing the power they have over me. So in that sense, CEOs are like God. And from what I understand, they like it that way.

Maybe, just maybe the system is planned (liberals would say rigged) in favor of the rich. However, I'd like to see the proof of this without it getting all complicated with a bunch of charts, numbers and math. My motto: if your argument can't fit within a fortune cookie, it's too complicated for me to listen to. That's why a phrase like "Let's take our country back" works so well for people like me. How do you argue with that?

But if the rich have an extra advantage, then it's because they deserve it. By making money, they earn the breaks the rest of us don't get. So they can then earn more money. And then earn more of those breaks. This never-ending cyclical cause & effect system is virtually flawless. But wealthy Americans don't like it when you point this advantage out. So forget I said anything, except to say the system is AWESOME!

However, we can do our part to help the rich out. It's the least we can do for them.

First we must eradicate all the overbearing, big-government regulations that get in the way of profit. Sure these regulations may save a few lives, but they also cost companies much of the capital they need to invest. And part of that investment could very well include jobs. You never know.

"Invest" is a word that CEOs and politicians use a lot. It's a positive-sounding word, full of business-speak. It's inspiring. It shows that the people who use that word really know what they're doing. Liberals would say that "invest" is a loaded, generalized word, where an "investment" could technically include a $200,000 velvet painting of Elvis for the CEO's personal bathroom.

Now, which regulations are the most harmful to business growth? I don't know, but I trust the smartest guys in the room, the business owners, to have those answers and have our best interests at heart. Because without us workers, where would they be? They need us. And their way of saying thanks is in our paychecks. It's in our vacation and sick days. It's in the way the HR representative hints at remorse when they fire us.

Second… actually, there is no second. This is just a quick chapter on ending regulations that stifle business growth. Regulations like ensuring clean(ish) air, comfortable workplaces, lighting that only flickers at a 10 flicks/minute pace, and twice daily bathroom breaks. In fact, regulations that protect workers only make workers weaker. If only the strongest workers survive (literally), then we're assured the strongest workforce. And as the weaklings perish, it opens up more job opportunities for everyone else. Fewer job candidates = a smaller pool of worker competition. So the sacrifice is worth it.

CHAPTER 28
Elizabeth Warren: The Devil

Boy the liberals sure love this Elizabeth Warren chick. She's a pal of Obama, too. So she's on my List. My List of People Who Piss me Off. It has a few hundred names on it, but for this book, I only devote chapters to a select few. So you know they're the ones who REALLY piss me off. Elizabeth is in my Piss Me Off Hall of Fame.

The Bible says the devil will be disguised as a nice person (I'm paraphrasing a bit). That's why I'm always skeptical of nice, pleasant people. If you tell me to "Have a nice day," I'll give you the stink-eye. If you say, "Nice to meet you," I'll tell you to piss off. If you tell me my kids are cute, I'll have them kick you in the shins.

Elizabeth Warren comes across as a nice person, acting all concerned for consumers and wanting to protect them from predatory lenders. Ergo, she's the devil. Unless you don't believe in the Bible.

But I don't need Lizzie here protecting me. Thanks but no thanks! I can protect myself! Like most sensible people, I can spot a predatory lender easily. It's like gaydar, but for predatory lenders. And I'll give you my secrets on knowing who's predatory:

1. They have a small office with bad lighting
2. They wear old, shortsleeve button up shirts.
3. They have a comb-over.
4. They talk like a used car salesman.
5. They chew gum and/or a toothpick.
6. They have a secretary who wears too much makeup, high heels, and fake blonde hair.
7. They say "I don't know" when you ask what "APR" is.
8. They work out of the back of a van or Chevette.

The rest of the lenders? They're legit. You can trust them. And if they're backed by a bank or brokerage firm (with their very own website), all the better.

See, we don't need Elizabeth Warren to protect us. We can protect ourselves. Seriously, those guys at Citi and Chase and Bank of America... sure they have thousands of people whose sole purpose is to craft loan and credit conditions designed to take as much money as possible from me, using jargon I couldn't hope to understand. But I have my instincts, and I think I can handle myself against them. Even if I'm not really sure how a variable rate works, I'm sure the nice woman at the bank will set me straight.

Republicans and conservatives don't like Elizabeth either. I think it's because they know if her crazy ideas take root in the collective consciousness, people will want to see them enacted, and that makes conservatives less powerful. And who wants that?

Now Elizabeth is running for Senate. I guess she couldn't take the heat of being rejected as head of the Consumer Protection Bureau she founded. So what all of us Americans can do is make sure she doesn't get elected. And if we do our parts, we accomplish this quite easily. First, we all move to Massachusetts. Then we register to vote. Then we vote for sexy smooth Scott Brown instead. He wins, Elizabeth gets depressed and jumps off a bridge. And then Elizabeth Warren will no longer piss me off.

CHAPTER 29
Calling those you don't agree with "parasites" really gets a reaction

I'm not a big proponent of name-calling. Unless it's absolutely necessary. Or accurate. Or feels like the right thing to do in the heat of the moment. And calling a liberal or Democrat a "parasite" gets them angry. Which makes it OK.

Also, conservatives are much better at name-calling than liberals. Because Glenn Beck ("Obama is a racist who hates white people"), Rush Limbaugh ("Halfrican"), and Ann Coulter ("Bill Clinton molested the help.") among others have told us that it's OK to be mean. Name-calling isn't just for the playground, or on anonymous comments sections. Anyone can (and should) do it!

Besides being a party that gets things done, Republicans have gotten name-calling down to a science. And liberals always react. They can't ignore it. So it totally gets them off their game. Instead of trying to make a point, they find themselves reacting to the name-calling, and by the time they get back on topic, the segment is over and the host (let's say it's Bill O'Reilly) has moved on to talking about his book. (Thanks for looking out for us!)

Here's an example of how you can knock a liberal off their game. Imagine I'm on "The Factor®™©" debating Al Franken.

Me: That is why liberals are destroying this country.

Al: If we could get back on topic for a second. The minimum wage needs to be raised. This is especially true when Walmart has become our country's number one job source, and most of their jobs are at or near minimum wage. If minimum wage jobs are to become the main source of income for people, it needs to be higher.

Me: You're a parasite Jew.

Al: Excuse me.

Me: You heard me. I know you can't see me through those thick glasses, but you heard me, you parasite Jew.

Al: I really don't think this is appropriate. Bill...?

Bill (host): I'll allow it.

Me: Boo-yah!

And suddenly, Al Franken has lost his argument. He got so distracted by my name-calling (and who'd have thought Al Franken was Jewish? It was a lucky guess on my part.) that he lost his train of thought. Any point he was trying to make is out the window.

So it's good that liberals are so easily distracted. Here's my tip: any time it feels like a liberal has some momentum in their argument, or if it seems like they're making a good point, strike back with an outrageous claim or some name-calling. They can't help but react to it. Some examples:

"Obama is worse than Hitler."

"Douchebag."

"Parasite."

"Dumbass!"

"Pauly D"

"Paulie Shore"

"Commie."

"I hope you get lupus."

"Let me know when you say something relevant."

"I'm sleeping with your wife/husband/longtime companion!"

"Dickless moron" (works better on guys)

"Get a job and a bath."

"Homo says what?"

Note, my next book will be nothing but stuff like this.

CHAPTER 30
All this typing is hurting my fingers

Just wanted you to know.

But the sacrifice is worth it. Pain is temporary. Obama's poopy pants are forever.

CHAPTER 31
How can voter fraud be a "myth" when there are dozens of cases of it each year?

People died giving us the right to vote. It is essentially the one thing that gives us citizens a voice in the democratic process. It is the one thing that, when practiced correctly, can make the greatest difference in the direction our country takes. Which is why we must make it as difficult as possible to do.

Voting is a privilege. Not a right.

Voter fraud is rampant in this country, and must be stopped. Example: the state of Kansas had 221 cases of voter fraud since 1997. That is over 12 per year! 12! In one state! And what's most shocking is that a lot of those cases are just "misunderstandings" (a parent trying to vote for a kid away at college, for example), which makes this fraud all the more devious. Because it shows that fraud takes many forms, and goes deeper than one realizes. If it's so easy to accidentally commit voter fraud, imagine how easy it is to commit voter fraud on purpose.

Some say that requiring photo IDs, getting rid of early voting and making registration more difficult is just the Republicans' way of suppressing voters (such as the poor, blacks and Hispanics, college students, women, Democrats) who would tend to vote Democrat. That is sheer lunacy. Lunacy supported by facts. And as we all know, facts are stupid (see Chapter 2).

Because when you look at the people who vote Democrat, they tend to be the people *you don't want voting*. They're just not qualified to vote. It's like letting the hospital janitor perform open-heart surgery. These unqualified voters don't see things the right way. They've drunk the Kool-aid, and because of that they're basing their votes on falsehoods. For example, they don't believe that tax cuts pay for themselves. And they vote based on that belief. We're actually putting our country in danger by letting Democrats vote!

Look at it this way. If your dad is about to take out the car, and he believes that he should drive on the LEFT SIDE of the road, would you give him your keys? Of course not. The same holds true for letting people vote Democrat. They're just hurting themselves, and others. Think of Republicans in this story as the family in the minivan driving on the right side of the road, who you dad crushes and kills. Yep, it is that serious. You let someone vote Democrat, and we die. Plus there is no seatbelt or airbag to protect us from people that vote Democrat. Only death awaits.

It's a no-brainer. We must make voting more difficult in order to make voter fraud less likely. The harder we make it to vote (show six forms of ID, be white, be conservative, be a millionaire, go to church twice a week), the harder it is to commit voter fraud. And that's important. And if voting is really tough to do, then only the people who truly care about voting will get to do it. If climbing Mt. Everest were easy, everyone would do it. It's the same thing with voting. Make it difficult, and *it means something.*

This country was founded on ideals like voting. Soldiers died to give us that right. We declared independence from England to make it happen. So I understand when people say that restricting voting demeans that sacrifice. I respectfully disagree. Totally. And unequivocally. Because that kind of thinking is downright stupid.

To me, voter fraud is what undermines that sacrifice. Would our soldiers feel right about dying so some ACORN liberals can commit voter fraud? Soldiers did not die to let voter fraud happen. So by taking away voting, we can take away voter fraud. It's like prohibition. We took away the booze, and people stopped drinking.

CHAPTER 32

His Middle Name is Hussein for cryin' out loud!

The United States put a man with the middle name of Hussein in the White House. Just when I thought liberals couldn't get any dumber, they prove me wrong once again. Sometimes I think this nation is too stupid to get the great leaders it deserves. But all I can do is point out the obvious, hope enough people come to realize it, and we can take this country back. From Obama. And the stupid poopy pants he wears.

Now I can understand how millions looked past his funny name and ended up voting for the guy. He makes a nice speech. He doesn't seem threatening. He's got a nice smile and a good jump shot.

But like my pastor told me, behind every smile is a set of teeth. Then he laughed manically as his eyes turned yellow. Which seemed strange, but hey, he's a pastor, so it must have been OK.

Obama reminds me of Gus from "Breaking Bad." Now if you never have seen the show, here's a quick synapsis. A public school chemistry teacher named Walt starts cooking crystal meth (our tax dollars at work!) and before long his primo product attracts the attention of a big time meth dealer named Gus, played by the wonderfully talented Giancarlo Esposito. Gus runs his meth business through a fast food chicken franchise. To the general public he's this nice, caring man. He gives to charity. He works the front counter. He dresses well. He's kind of black.

But when he goes into meth dealer mode, he's a ruthless killer, murdering children, cutting the throats of associates, and poisoning the cartel. The resemblance to Obama is just uncanny.

Because Gus, like Obama, hides in plain sight. And because of this, one would never suspect him of being a murderous meth dealer or someone who wants to destroy America. It's the perfect disguise.

His only slip-up? His middle name. He thought we would never find out what it was. But we did. And now the house of cards he built is about to come crashing down. Thanks to conservatives like me who discovered the truth, who discovered that his middle name is code for "bad guy".

Now I don't want to make any crazy assertions here, but I think this info is proof that Obama and Saddam Hussein are brothers. Or at the very least, cousins. Because Hussein is not a common name. It's not like Johnson or Smith or Williams. So it can't be a coincidence. These two had to be related. So no wonder Obama voted against the Iraq war. He didn't want us attacking his brother!

What's in a name? Well in Obama's case, it's a dictatorship.

Yep, it truly is scary to think about.

CHAPTER 33
Jeremiah Wright and Bill Ayers. Obama's BFFs

You can judge a person by the company he keeps. And in Obama's case, you can judge a president by the company he used to keep on occasion.

First, the Reverend. I never went to Jeremiah Wright's freakshow disguised as a church. But Obama did, for 20 years! And we all know that priests, pastors, rabbis and whatever you call a Muslim guy in the pulpit have more influence on their followers than ANYBODY. So after 20 years of listening to Wright, it makes sense that Obama would become a mindless robot, doing the reverend's bidding. Like "goddamning America." That's right. Based on the one clip of Jeremiah Wright that I've seen (and really, it's just the snippit they show on Fox News every day), the reverend said to "God damn America!" That's right. He swore in church. And that swearword was sandwiched between the two greatest words of all time. That's just sad.

So of course, Obama would devote his life to "goddamning America." And damn us he did. With healthcare, and bringing troops home, and job-creation bills. Thanks a lot, Reverend.

Meanwhile, Bill Ayers bombed a building back in the 1970s, long before he even met Obama. And back in Obama's Chicago days, Ayers hosted a party for Obama. Now I don't know about you, but only one person has ever thrown me a party. My mom. No one else.

What does that mean? That in America, only your best friends (like my mom) throw parties for each other. So anyone that says Williams Ayers was an acquaintance of Obama doesn't know what he's talking about. Obviously the two are best buds (or maybe something more, though I don't want to speculate. gay).

So Obama's best friend is a bomb-throwing maniac. That's real nice.

But what's most important is that Obama obviously condones this kind of behavior. Maybe you can't be friends with Obama unless you bomb buildings. And Obama has so many crazy fans that they may try to bomb buildings to become friends with him. Just imagine... an epidemic of building-bombing across this great nation of ours, all because Obama pals around with terrorists.

My proposal... Obama is not allowed to have any friends. Shut down his Facebook account. Nobody can say anything nice to him or about him.

If we all become Obama's enemy, we'll be fine.

CHAPTER 34
Yelling at my TV is good cardio

I yell at my TV on a regular basis, and I feel just as tired after doing that as most people do after the Chest & Back routine from P90X.

I yell at most stations. Fox News on occasion (Shut up, Shepard Smith! Why don't they just "shepard" you outta there? HA! Did I use that joke already? So what? It's good enough to be repeated). CNN regularly (Santa Blitzer, why are you always on?). MSNBC constantly (Burn in hell, everybody, even Joe

Scarborough). And even Nickelodeon gets under my skin and needs a good yelling-to (I don't care if your dad is fighting in Afghanistan, iCarly, you and your web show just piss me off. It's not always that funny!).

So when it comes to yelling at your TV, make sure you have some oxygen nearby, so you don't get lightheaded. And speaking of Oxygen, when is the new season of Tori and Dean gonna start? I haven't yelled at Tori Spelling in months! And make sure your remote batteries are always fresh, so you can flip like a pro.

Here's a quick guide on who and what to yell at:

ESPN: Everybody, especially Mark Schlereth.
ESPN2: Everybody, especially Mark Schlereth. And Skip Bayless. And good luck trying to outyell Herm Edwards.
FX: Shia Lebeouf in Transformers
BET: Anyone white
Lifetime: Swoosie Kurtz
VH1: Nobody... just sway to the music.
MTV: The TEEN MOMS!
A&E: Jerry Orbach
History: Adolf Hitler
Travel: Food, when Man is vs it.
Comedy Central: Cartman
Disney: Anyone on "Shake It Up"
Animal Planet: Those stupid elephants
TBS: Jim Halpert on Tuesdays, Stewey on Wednesdays, and Tyler Perry the rest of the week.
TNT: Bones
USA: Mr. Burn Notice.
BRAVO: Salmon Rushdie's ex-wife

CHAPTER 35
Let's Take Care of America First! (with tax cuts)

A great man once said: "Charity begins at home."

That great man died rich and alone in his apartment.

But the sentiment of his words still rings true. Before we give money to starving children in Africa, we should first see if there are some starving bank accounts here that could use the money more. And if you watch Fox Business Channel, there usually is.

Let me give you a real-world example. When you get on a plane, the stewardess (sorry, that's not politically correct anymore. I meant to say "flight bitch") goes through the safety checklist, and one of those items is what to do in a sudden loss of cabin pressure. This is important to know, because I've seen a lot of movies where this happens. Some guy with an itchy trigger finger shoots off his gun in a crowded plane, and all the air gets sucked out, people panic, and then they regret that they didn't listen to the honey-buns drink wench before takeoff. But what do they tell you? To put the oxygen mask on YOURSELF before placing it on your child. I used to think this was because grown-ups have jobs and are more productive members of society than children, so we need them more. But actually it's because you can't help the child until you help yourself first. The kid won't be helped if you pass out.

The same holds true with foreign aid. We must first take care of all our country's problems (paying off the debt, making our air and water 100% clean, reducing the tax rate to zero, school uniforms for all, removing HGH from all sports, and making sure everyone has at least one job, to name a few). After we handle that, which should take about 20 minutes without the Democrats' "help", THEN we can give some cash to other countries. Otherwise, we're just that adult passed out in Seat 23B (because the kid INSISTED on taking the window seat), while the child in 24A fails to understand a life-saving device that works much like a Halloween mask.

In fact, since we're the country everyone else goes to for a hand-out, it really doesn't seem fair. It's always GIVE GIVE GIVE with us. Well wake up, world! We're not some Scrooge on Christmas morning tossing out dollar bills and hard candies. Nope, we're going to be more like Scrooge before he had all those bad dreams. Scrooge, mixed a little bit with the Class Bully.

That's why other countries should pay us "protection money". With great power comes great responsibility. And with great power comes the ability to shove other countries into a locker until they give up their lunch money. If you don't want bombed, pay the piper. Oh, and if we ever did anything nice for you (Iraq, remember all that freedom we dropped on you?), pay us double. France would be speaking German if not for us, so they get a bill. And don't pay us in snails.

The way I see it, there are over 300 countries in the world. That's a lot of cash flow sources for us. Send them each a bill for us not bombing them, and we could take care of our problems sooner. Then we can give them some foreign aid.

Israel is the exception. Our nuke plans (and a lot of checks) are in the mail, you guys.

CHAPTER 36
We caught Osama. Whatever.

Do you know how long Obama was president before we caught Osama Bin Laden? Almost three years! Unbelievable. And it was nearly ten years after 9/11. I have to ask, what was Obama waiting for?

And really, by the time we caught him (and let's be honest, Obama had nothing to do with it. It was the work of brave Navy Seals... like Charlie Sheen and Michael Biehn in "Navy Seals," or Demi Moore in "GI Jane"), no one really cared. Osama was all played out. It was like the fourth Indiana Jones movie. The last sequel was at least 15 years too late. So America just shrugged (but not like Atlas) at the release of "Kingdom of the Crystal Skull". Just like we all shrugged when they caught Osama. Like, whatever. In fact, I forgot we were still looking for him. But the next thing I know, Obama is on my TV at the must-see-TV hour of 11pm Sunday night, telling us that Osama had been killed. Thanks for interrupting "The Apprentice", Mr. Show-off!

So that was big news for awhile, and then the liberal media gave us some Photoshopped footage of people, presumably Americans, cheering in the streets. I looked out my window. No one was dancing on my cul de sac.

What bugs me the most is how Obama took ALL the credit. He was thumping his chest like he was king of the castle. He probably demanded some "Caught Osama Sex" from Michelle.

Well guess what, Bush deserves most of the credit. Bush is like the smooth quarterback who threw the bomb, the long bomb that spiraled in the air for 9 years. Obama was the hotheaded wide receiver who only caught the ball placed RIGHT IN HIS HANDS. So while Bush is all cool and just jogging to the sidelines, Obama is doing some fancy little touchdown dance and Lambeau leap to the adoring fans.

And it was the same thing with Khadafi. The Libyans took down their dictator on their own, but Obama is in front of the cameras, taking all the credit. Sure he said it was mostly the work of the Libyan people, but we know what he really meant. That he is King Awesome, bringing down bad guys like Alex Laughton on "Hawaii 5-0".

Oh, and then Kim Jung Il died, of natural causes. So Obama makes a big ol' speech about that. As if Obama gave him that heart attack. Maybe if Obama would gloat a little bit less, we could have enjoyed their deaths a little more. Because it's no fun breakdancing on a grave when one guy hogs the cardboard.

So in conclusion... Osama, Khadafi, Il, Mubarak, their deaths and/or removals from office don't mean anything. In fact, the voids they leave behind will be worse than their dictatorships. Why? Because we didn't go to war to remove them, and replace them with successors picked by yours truly. That's how the system is supposed to work. So I would go so far as to say that Osama's death is a bad thing. Way to go, Obama! You sure screwed up this time. When it comes to satisfying us conservatives, you fail every time.

CHAPTER 37
George Clooney: One ugly son of a bitch

This guy. What is with this guy? He has it all... looks, money, women. Why would he want to get involved with the liberals and their cause? What's with all the belly-aching about Darfur? Why would he campaign for Obama? Is Clooney stupid too?

Well, he *is* an actor. It doesn't take a Mensa member to become one of those. Just memorize a few lines, be all dramatic when the camera is on, and cash a big fat paycheck. I could be an actor. An even better actor than Clooney. But I think the world would prefer that I always be the real me... all the time. Unlike Clooney, I don't have to escape the drudgery of real life by becoming someone else in front of a movie camera.

But Clooney is just one of a ton of Hollywood liberals. Obviously you don't become famous in entertainment without being liberal. They kick you out otherwise. It's one of the questions they ask before you get your SAG card. And that's why movies have such a liberal slant to them. Like "All the President's Men." A story about a couple of crusading, liberal journalists trying to take down a Republican president. For liberals and the liberal media, that movie is porn.

Sure, we had some ass-kicking movies back in the glory days of Reagan. Most of the First Bloods. All the best Jean Claude Van Damme (He's French, but he kicked ass). The American Ninja Series. And Chuck Norris. And Charles Bronson. They proved what the rest of the world suspected... that one tough American is all it takes to win a war. And kill you all dead.

But while us conservatives loved the action, Hollywood stayed liberal. And this point is proven every four years, when the music, movie and television industry seem to come out (not in the Hollywood gay way) en masse for the Democrat candidate. How do you know it's a presidential year? Martin Sheen is talking behind a podium.

Democrats get all the actors I want to like but can't because of their liberal views. And it kind of pisses me off. So who am I left with? Jon Cryer and Kelsey Grammer. That's about it. The aforementioned Chuck Norris may pop up. But if I'm being honest, the only working conservative actors we got are Bucky and Frasier. And I can only catch Kelsey Grammer on the STARZ network, and I'm not paying $10.95/month for that. Not until Spartacus shows more boobs and less pecs.

The problem with Hollywood is that its actors are portrayed as "cool." And kids look up to actors. And when they find out actors are liberal, kids may think being liberal is "cool." Well guess what, kids! Most actors are struggling to make ends meet, waiting tables and living with six roommates and dressing up as dildos in underground sex plays just to earn a few bucks. Does that sound cool?

Does it sound cool to have to sleep with the director to get a speaking role? What if that director was Woody Allen?

Does it sound cool to hear critics like Roger Ebert say your performance was flat, or to have TMZ print a picture with a drawn arrow pointing to your "flabby" stomach as you bend to pick something up at the beach?

Does it sound cool to adopt 15 kids from Africa?

That's the truth behind Hollywood. It's a corrupt city where everyone commits the seven deadly sins before 7am, and breaks all 10 commandments before 10am. It's a city that would be more beautiful if it were on fire. It's populated by zombies hungry for a script. It's not cool. It's liberal.

CHAPTER 38
Stem Cells. But I'm not buyin'.

This hasn't been a hot topic for about 10 years. So I'm bringing it back, and I'm wearing my Swatch watch as I do it.

Now stem cells were a big deal in Bush's first term. He wrestled with the decision on whether federal funds should go to the study of stem cells, which showed promise in treating an array of deadly and excruciating ailments.

But there was a catch. The best stem cells came from babies. That you had to kill.

It was the classic dilemma. A chance to extend the lives of those already living, by sacrificing the lives of those who would never get to live in the first place. And Socrates thought he answered the big questions.

So only a man as wise as Bush could take on this dilemma. After wrestling with it for months (which really showed us how much he was wrestling with it), he came to a compromise. Those cells already being studied would get some money. Anything else... find you own way. When it came to solutions, Bush was like King Solomon. He wouldn't let people cut babies in half.

While I may never be able to stop the baby massacre genocide that is stem cell research... after all I am but one person. But I can take a stand against stem cell research. And that stand is this: I will never use any of the medicinal advancements that are the result of stem cell research, except on one condition: if it can improve the quality of, or extend, my life and the lives of my loved ones. That's it! In all other cases, I refuse to let the benefits of stem cell research benefit me.

Because stem cells come from *babies*! Snowflake babies.

You don't remember snowflake babies? These are the frozen embryos who found adoptive parents. Dozens of these snowflake babies are now snowflake kids and snowflake teenagers, who by now probably hate the term "snowflake" but who must endure it for PR purposes.

And with tens of thousands of these potential snowflake babies in fertility clinic freezers across the country, it's a dandy opportunity to adopt one! I would do it, but I don't have enough money, plus I'm a little too old to raise kids again. But don't let me stop you. Go get yourself a snowflake!

And has anyone thought of the dire consequences of stem cell research? Have you seen "Species"? Or the countless sequels that followed it? You don't mess with nature. You don't try to alter God's plan. And God would not plan on having the death of babies create cures for insidious diseases. Not our God.

If you ask me, such research would backfire horribly (once again, see "Species". Because Natasha Henstridge is HOT), and the cure would be worse than the disease. Don't say I never warned you. Of course, we'll all be dead, so you'd be unable to say I didn't want you. But you get the idea.

CHAPTER 39
In America it's awesome to be poor and it sucks to be rich.

Poor people sit around and do nothing except get drunk and drink beer. They choose to be poor. And that's a stupid choice.

Or is it?

Maybe poor people are brilliant. Because the government (with our tax dollars!) just gives them Cadillacs, Xboxes, suitcases full of cash, and beer stamps. All for sitting on their asses and not working.

They flaunt their refrigerators, and microwaves, and VCRs and toasters as if they're Gloria freakin' Vanderbilt.

These people aren't poor. Not if they have toasters and vacuum cleaners lying around. My definition of poor is having NOTHING. No food, no water, no clothing, no shelter, no pot to piss in. You eat dirt. If you're lucky. If you're truly poor, that means no purchase you can make brings you any sort of joy or satisfaction. Then, and only then, can you receive government assistance. For 10 days. And you must pay it back with 70% interest within three years.

I'm a compassionate man. That's why I want to help those who are truly poor. The ones who are so poor they can't afford a pen with which to fill out the government assistance form. Unfortunately, it's the "so-called poor" (they're not even homeless) who ruin it for the real poor. I would love to help the homeless man that eats garbage to survive. But how can I be sure that my tax dollars go to him, and not some freeloading family living in a new refrigerator box? And I would rather have my money go no place than risk it going to the wrong place.

And the reason for this is simple: paying taxes is worse than having your balls pureed in a blender. So no one wants to see his tax dollars wasted. And no one pays more taxes than the rich.

I pay my fair share of taxes, probably about $9000 per year. And I hate it. Every dollar I lose to the government causes me to weep. So think of the poor billionaire who pays tens of thousands, or even millions of dollars in taxes. What suffering! Is this how we punish rich people for working so hard? Are we animals?

Yet we still squeeze every last drop from the rich. They pay the most, and we ask them to pay more. Their "fair share" as Obama puts it. No wonder no one wants to be rich anymore.

Imagine the so-called wealthy man, sitting in his library writing yet another big check to the government so an inner city kid can eat brand-name cereal. What goes on in that man's mind? If it were me, I'd be thinking: "This library would be a whole lot bigger if not for all these taxes."

Or maybe he could create a job. But NO. Obama's spend-until-you-drop government won't let a job creator create jobs. Yet still these 1%-ers persevere, creating jobs when they can, while only adjusting the wages to offset the incredible price he must pay.

While I'm not what they call "rich", I try to do my part for job creation. I know it's cliché to tell a pan handler or hobo or homeless person to just "get a job." But that's what I do. Tough love. Give a man a fish, he'll eat for a day. Teach him to fish, and he eats for a lifetime. But I don't have time to teach. Someone else will have to do it. But by not giving him any fish, the threat of starvation means he'll be forced to learn! Somehow. It's like dunking a basketball. If you point a gun at someone's head and say, "Dunk," they'll find a way if they have the commitment and drive.

Now when I tell these hobos to "Get a job," I mean at a place where I don't work. Because hobos are icky and gross and addicted to drugs. So the company where I work shouldn't hire him. But I'm sure there's a company out there that will hire him to sweep floors. Like many conservatives, I truly believe that millions of floor-sweeping jobs are just there for the taking, but they go unfilled because the hobos are too proud or lazy to take them.

It's why we need our corporations to be bigger, not smaller. Too big to fail? I say not big enough! The bigger the company, the more jobs they have, from floorsweeper on up to CEO.

This country was founded on growth. From day one it's been all about growing and expanding. We started with 13 colonies and grew to 50 states, 36 of which are awesome. The NFL is now 32 teams (if you include the Jaguars). CEOs make a lot more money. Houses are bigger. Kids are fatter. So it makes sense that capitalism follows the same "Bigger is Better" principle.

So when liberals gripe that banks are too big too fail, what they mean is, "I'm jealous because I'm poor." They're just mad at the banks that don't want liberals working for them. And the phrase "too big to fail" is right on the money. Because these companies are so amazing, they're unable to fail. They'll always succeed, as long as they keep getting bigger.

But Obama sticks his middle finger to the big businesses and rich people, blaming them (Mr. Blame does it again, when he's not apologizing for America) when he should be blaming the poor people who won't get off the couch to work because tax payers like me are supporting their addiction to big-screen TVs. And cassette decks.

What happens when Obama's policies mean we don't have any more rich people? What will the rest of us aspire to? We *need* to lavish wealth and riches on the lucky few, not just because they earned it, but because it inspires the rest of us to try and get rich. We *need* those people to have fancy cars, huge yachts, mansions in the hills, private islands, and harems. It provides a visual goal for the rest of us. It spurs us to become rich. Now most of us will fail miserably, but at least we tried. And if you tried your best, then you can lie on your deathbed and die happy. And in an incredible amount of debt.

CHAPTER 40
I'll vote for a woman if she's pretty

Sarah Palin. Nikki Hailey. Christine O'Donnell. Michele Bachmann when the light hits her just right. These are all strong, ambitious and attractive women whom I would vote for if given the chance. It's proof that conservatives do have headstrong women that also know their place. And they're pretty. They better be pretty. Otherwise we won't listen. Remember Barbara Mikulski? Neither do I.

I don't even care how big their boobs are. I'm more of a face-man. That's how open-minded I am. I don't even notice boob size in politics. It's hard to, because their wardrobes kind of hide it. It's hard to scope out "candidate cleavage" on the campaign trail when they insist on wearing pantsuits. Besides, once a nipple makes an appearance, that campaign is toast. So girl candidates have to button up the twins.

But all things being equal, I will vote for the pretty woman over the less attractive woman in the primary (provided that no man is running), and then vote for her over the Democrat in the general election.

Yet it's the conservatives who are seen as chauvinists keeping women down, just because we don't think they should be paid as much as men, and because we don't think they should get maternity leave, or decide what to do with their bodies, and because we want them making our meals and fetching our beer and finding us men physically attractive no matter what, and because we don't want them to vote, or drive, or look out the window, or learn to read and write. But if you're a pretty, conservative woman, you can do anything. Maybe even become vice-president of the United States.

That, my friends, is Girl Power.

CHAPTER 41
Global Warming. Schmobal Warming.

Global warming was a failure. How do I know? Because the liberals now call it "climate change." So I guess that new phrasing gives them more "leeway" when they talk about it. Like when we get a blizzard in October and someone from our side logically points out. "Look at all this GLOBAL WARMING! Al Gore is stupid."

However, the liberals don't need to school me on the complexities of global warming or climate change or hocus pocus or whatever they call it these days. I get the gist... that off-weather occurrences are the result of climate change. But here's what the liberals won't tell you: It's not that big a deal.

According to them, if the average global temperature rises by two or three degrees in the next 50 years, it'll be a catastrophe. Icebergs will melt, we'll get more hurricanes, and the dead will walk the earth. Ooohhh, I'm real scared.

Let me explain why I'm not shaking in my boots. Yesterday in my hometown, the high was 54 and the low was 35. That's a difference of 19 DEGREES in one 24-hour period. And guess what? The glaciers didn't melt. Manhattan wasn't flooded. Al Gore's face didn't fall off (He invented the Internet. HA!).

So if a 19-degree fluctuation in one day doesn't trigger the end of the world, how is a three-degree change in 50 years going to do it? It stuns me that we give scientists any credit at all!

Oh, and don't get me started on how, if global warming is real, mankind caused it. That's impossible. In summertime, I keep my air conditioning on full blast, even when I'm not home. I'm actually COOLING things down. So how does *that* make things hotter?

Yet Obama says we need to conserve energy, we need to recycle and all that crap. But if we recycle, then all those people whose job it is to manufacture cans and plastic and metal will lose their jobs! Way to go, Mr. Stupid Poopy Pants Job Destroyer! And why do we need to recycle pop cans anyway? That's gross. I don't want to use a can someone else already drank from. And did you see that some toilet paper is made from recycled products? Ewwww.

Besides, it's not worth the risk of spending millions and billions of dollars to save the planet, if there's no proof that the planet will be destroyed in the first place. It's a waste of time and money. Sure, eating fast food every day may lead to heart disease, but I don't KNOW that's going to happen. So why spend any of my money on salad?

Climate change is just another "scare tactic" that is about as real as the Boogeyman. And if the world does get any hotter, I'll just turn up my AC.

CHAPTER 42
More disturbing facts

I got these true facts from underground sources. Which means they came to me while sitting in my basement.

• Obama chews with his mouth open.
• He thinks Cheryl Ladd is the best of the Charlie's Angels.
• He thinks he's the Messiah. That title belongs to Ronald Reagan.
• He never puts the car keys back on the hook like he's supposed to.
• He's got a maniacal laugh.
• He's got access to the Button.
• He doesn't say enough nice things about Sarah Palin.
• He voted for himself in the 2008 presidential election.
• He sings off-key in the shower.
• You never see him at any Tea Party rallies.
• He smashed your pumpkins.
• He picked a Democrat as his running mate.
• He goes on more vacations than I do.
• He never pulls his weight in the carpool.
• He gave Solyndra a loan they didn't pay back.
• He also took credit for the death of Bob Hope's wife.
• He doesn't even drive himself anywhere.
• He's got his own plane.
• He's the Son of Sam.
• He's responsible for about 50% of all serious crimes that have been committed in the last 25 years.
• Mel Gibson didn't go crazy until Obama became president. Just sayin'.
• He can't juggle, but says he can.
• He once tried to re-enact the complete Saw series at the White House. If you don't believe me, ask yourself, "Where's Donnie Wahlberg?"
• He doesn't buy cologne. He just rubs on free samples from GQ and Vanity Fair and Details.

- He's building a doomsday device.
- He always takes the last cookie.
- He makes fun of those with diabetes.
- He drinks light beer.
- He apologizes for America.
- He's doing nothing about SkyNet.

CHAPTER 43
He is the Antichrist, or something worse.

Did you know that Obama has been the first president EVER to be called the Antichrist on a regular basis? Is that a coincidence, or is it fact?

Where there's smoke, there's fire. And where there's fire, there's Hell. And that's where Obama is from.

So if enough people say Obama is the Antichrist, shouldn't that claim at least be investigated? Doesn't it deserve some merit? If the claim really was hogwash (as liberals contend), then why haven't other presidents been called the Antichrist? Hmmm. Oh, I guess if you make an accusation about Obama, it must be a lie! Way to have an open mind, liberals! You're all a bunch of atheists anyway. What do you know about religion and the Antichrist? Let the conservatives who are true Christians decide. We'd appreciate it if you'd respect our decision.

Guess what? When the Antichrist comes, he won't look like Hellboy. He'll look like a nice, harmless man. Because the devil is that shrewd. He's not going to show up acting like some asshole. It would totally blow his cover. So instead he arrives with no known birthplace and has a mother from Kansas (not unlike Superman). And the only clues we have that he could be the devil is the way he wants to destroy America.

That, my friends, is our secret weapon. American ideals are the OPPOSITE of evil. So when Obama forces people to buy health insurance that would murder Grandma, he's showing his hand. Or should I say "claw." Every time he announces some anti-American (and therefore Pro-Devil) idea, it's more evidence that proves he's the Antichrist.

That's how us conservatives can spot him for being the Devil. We don't wear the blinders that liberals wear. In fact, it's like we have those special glasses from 'They Live", which lets us see who the real bad guys are. And Obama is their king.

So how do we stop the Antichrist? I wish I had the right answer. Maybe an exorcism. But I'm not sure that's Constitutional. And trying to assassinate Obama? Too risky. Like they said on "The Usual Suspects": "How do you shoot the devil in the back. What if you miss?" And we can't wait around for Jesus to return in time. Obama's unleashing hellfire any day now.

I got it! Just make Obama's next coffee with Holy Water. Problem solved.

Except that means Joe Biden will take over. But I think he'd be a better alternative to the Antichrist.

CHAPTER 44
They closed Borders®, but illegals are still coming in! Obama's stupid immigration policy.

I thought we finally had some good news. Now when I heard last year they were closing borders, I got excited. Finally, maybe Obama wasn't the stupid poopy pants I had assumed. Well, my assumption on that assumption was wrong!

The borders that was closing was Borders®, the bookstore chain. Not the border we own and which we let Mexico look at once in awhile. So while I have nothing against Borders® (though I could have told them that trying to sell books when libraries just give them away for free is a terrible business idea), I do have a few opinions on what to do about The Border.

Now I'm not sure of the true stats, but I heard that there are 22 million illegal aliens here in the United States. That's the same number it was in 1987. So it took 25 years for us to wake up and realize what a huge problem this is! Shame on us!

Also I heard that the illegal aliens that come here are murderers. I got an email that broke down the numbers, and it said illegals account for tens of thousands of murders in the United States every year. It must be true. It was in my inbox!

Now I live in America's heartland, far from The Border. But ever since this immigration crisis became so important, (Thank you, Lou Dobbs), I notice more than ever the people who are or look Mexican. And each time I see them I can't help but think, "Illegal? Or just lost?"

Most of the time I'll see these people up high, fixing roofs. And I'm pissed because I know they're taking those jobs away from good, hardworking Amish people.

I also heard or read that our country will be 50% Hispanic by the end of an upcoming decade. That just isn't right. Imagine, a whole race of people coming into a country and taking it over as they push, for lack of a better word, us "Native Americans" off their land. It's sickening and unfair. And we can't let that happen to the United States.

So to be safe, we need to keep Hispanics out. Now some debate the number of Hispanics we should allow in this country. My opinion is that it should be zero. Just to be safe. That includes illegals and legals alike. Just wipe the slate clean. It may be difficult, moving the 22 million illegal aliens out, along with the rest of the people with Hispanic descent (so long, J. Lo), but if we want to be serious about Immigration Reform, we have to make the tough decisions and take on the tough tasks.

So how do we remove all these people? I don't know. I'm just a guy with solutions. Not a guy who enacts solutions. Perhaps we knock them out, like the A-Team did with B.A. Baracus when they wanted him to fly somewhere. We just give them all a little pill wrapped in a taco ("Here, take this. Yummy.") Then we put them in a big truck and drive them South of the Border, dropping them off in Ciudad Juarez. Then we sell their stuff on eBay. This process, if done right, should take a few weeks.

Another dilemma to the immigration problem is all the Anchor Babies, which by the way is such a beautiful title. Like Terror Babies. Needless to say it was Republican politicians who came up with such terms of endearment. And they say Republicans have no heart.

Anyway, these Anchor Babies are the ones who are born in the United States to illegals. Since they were born here, they're automatically citizens (all-time worst loophole). In fact, our open-door policy encourages a prego Hispanic to cross the border once her water breaks and give birth in a U. S. hospital. And since our hospitals can't turn them away (I guess it's bad PR to have women giving birth in the parking lot), the Anchor Babies are American Babies.

And these babies grow up to take our jobs. Shitty jobs, but still. At least give us the chance to reject cleaning a Days Inn first.

And even though they grow up in America, they still speak Spanish. Now like everyone else, I want a Constitutional amendment that makes English our official language. But we should go farther (or is it further), and make it the ONLY language spoken here. And no accents, either. Because if you don't talk English good, we don't want you. Besides, it makes us single-language-speaking Americans uncomfortable to hear others speaking a weird dialect. Because we know you're talking about us, saying things like, "Stupid American. I want you to die! And I will have sex with your daughter!" So if we could make English the only language, it would truly help us real Americans to relax.

Besides, they speak English EVERYWHERE! Even in Space. On "Star Wars", they spoke English. If they speak English on Alderon (which was a long time ago in a galaxy far, far away), they can damn well speak it in Alabama!

Now some liberal "thinkers" in Congress came up with the DREAM act. I don't know what it stands for, but it's a freakin' nightmare. It's amnesty with a fancy name. It works like this (I hope you haven't just eaten, because you'll throw up). It says that if a child of illegals gets a college degree or serves in the U.S. military, that resident will be given U.S.

citizenship. I hope you didn't vomit on your book. If so, no worries. Just buy a new copy.

Now liberals say this is a great law, because it ensures that the "best and brightest" of these kids will remain in this country and contribute to society. Once again, liberals are stupid.

The last thing we need is smarter people trying to take our jobs. It's hard enough competing with each other! But if the talent pool is larger and more talented, we're screwed! Finding a job will be harder than ever. It's like getting in a fight. You want your opponent to be smaller and weaker. And without hands and feet. Because working hard should be reserved for work, not finding work. That part should be easy.

Maybe we can put all the illegals in those abandoned Borders®.

CHAPTER 45
The only facts I need are the ones written by God.

God created the world, so yeah, He knows what He's doing. Until someone else can create the world, I'm going to believe what He says instead. If God says one thing and Wolf Blitzer says something else, I'm on God's side. And Wolf can enjoy burning in Hell.

When it comes to the Bible, I go with the NIV (New International Version). As a kid, we only had the St. James version, and it didn't make a lick of sense. With all the "thou's, sayeth's and unto's", it was like a Chinese menu, written in Chinese!

But about 10 years ago, I picked up the NIV, and it was much better. It reads more like a story, in plain readable English, with a true plot. It's like they took all the difficult, nonsense words from St. James, put a thesaurus to most of it, and came out with the NIV. So it all means the same thing, and the content is essentially the same. But it's easier to read. Thank God!

119

The NIV also has footnotes that provide some background to passages that might still be confusing. With all the characters to keep track of (it's like "Roots", or "The Girl with the Dragon Tattoo"), and all the cities with odd names, and all the potential contradictions, it's nice to have the footnotes to explain it all away. And the footnotes are the Word of God, too. Or they were inspired by God. Either way, it shows that details and proper citations are important to God. Which is good to know.

As a Christian, we focus mostly on the New Testament, the part with Jesus. However, Jesus doesn't make a big appearance, and that's disappointing. It's like Rodney Dangerfield in "Caddyshack". He totally steals every scene that he's in, but there's just not enough of him. He's only in four books, and they all have a similar take on the same story. So the Bible is 2,000 pages. And Jesus is on about 150. But Jesus makes quite the impression... he is The Man. In fact the whole Bible is all about him, like how the Star Wars saga is technically about Darth Vader. There's the rise, the fall (three of them) and resurrection of the main character.

First off, the whole Old Testament is about Jesus' arrival. There's the Creation, and early kingdoms, Noah and the ark, lots of smutty sin, and a bunch of guys whose names begin with "J". But the main parts that matter is when you read between the lines to discover the prophesy of Jesus's arrival, and his lineage. And the parts about gay people being an abomination. That matters, too. But for the most part, we just breeze through the Old Testament. It's the foundation... the back story, the prequel to The Epic Tale. Once you get past the Creation, Moses, and the Technicolor dreamcoat, the Old Testament isn't necessarily something to be read... it's just nice to know it's there. Like the foundation to your home. It's there, and that's what's important. Just knowing the Bible is loaded with chapters and verses that prove Obama is a big stupid poopy pants is enough.

The New Testament is where the story really picks up. Jesus is born, like the prophets foretold, and he spends three amazing years teaching, preaching and performing miracles before sacrificing himself in his prime. He was a rebel, who didn't follow anyone's rules (except his Father's). Just look at what made Jesus JESUS:

He gave free healthcare to the poor.

He broke bread with the persecuted.

He had dark skin.

He wanted peace.

He shared.

He spoke ill of the rich.

He was well-spoken.

Thousands of people came to hear him speak.

He was truly a great guy. If only we could have a president like Jesus!

I learned much of what's in the Bible at church and in Bible Study, which happens prior to a church service, or at a neighbor's house.

Bible Study is like a book blub. Though in this case you could call it Good Book Club. We start out talking about the Book, but after 15 minutes we're just gossiping. In this case, about stupid poopy pants Obama or high gas prices (his fault). But because it's a Bible study, we can't go completely off-target. For example, if we're studying letters from Paul, we can tie the Obama discussion back pretty easily. Ron *Paul* ran for president. Guess who *is* president? Obama! How dare the devil let him into our Bible study? Let's cast out the Obama demon by loudly complaining about him, one-upping each other with horror stories we heard last week on the comments section from NewsMax.

I'm a God-fearing man. Most of us Christians are. Why do we fear God? Because sometimes you can never guess what he'll do next. 40 days of rain? Why not! Locusts? Maybe! He's like a boss you don't want to anger. But if you do everything he says (and beg forgiveness when you don't), you'll be OK. God understands. But if you make Him mad, look out! That's why we fear God. Because we fear we'll screw up. We are imperfect after all. We're made in His image, but on the inside, we're way off!

And if we do something bad, then we damn well

brought it on ourselves. It's how He keeps us on our toes. Take the first example. God made Man imperfect. And when Man did something to show how imperfect he was (Adam and Eve eating the apple), he punished them. See, if Adam and Eve (and every generation after that) had just learned to LISTEN and be perfect the whole time, we'd still be in that Garden of Eden. But NO. Right off the bat, Adam and Eve screw it up. The very FIRST thing God tells them not to do, they do. I can only imagine God smacking himself in the forehead when He heard about this.

"What? Already? I thought it was an easy request! Don't eat the apple. Simple. The Garden is loaded with food! Great stuff too, most of it *better* than the apple. Orange groves, pineapples, easy access to meat. Couldn't the two of them have let me catch my breath a bit before disobeying me? I just spent a week creating the whole world, and two seconds after I say, 'Don't eat the apple,' THEY EAT THE APPLE! That's it… this is the last time I create a world with humans. Oh, and those two gotta leave the Garden. And the snake… I'll deal with him."

Now Obama really got us angry when he said that Christians "cling to religion". At first I thought it wasn't such a bad thing to say. Like maybe he meant it as a good thing, that we are committed to our faith. Nope, Sean Hannity cleared that up for me. It turns out Obama was belittling us and our faith, saying our shitty lives caused us to put our energies toward religion rather than bettering ourselves, that we let the more powerful people run all over us and accept it as long as we accept Christ. He was calling us weak. So it turns out Obama is an atheist who hates Christians.

I can deal with an atheist that will leave me be. An atheist leaves me alone, and I know he'll burn in Hell (H-E-Double-fuckin-hockey sticks) while I'm in Heaven. But Obama's total disdain for Christians is unforgivable. Yes, I cling to religion. In a good way. Not in the way Obama implies I do.

Fact about me: I dabbled in Catholicism for awhile. Now those guys are real big on ceremony. Mass is an hour long, and only about 10 minutes of it varies from week to week. It's like "Groundhog Day" in God's House.

Now Catholicism can be pretty strict. You sin, you go to Hell. But... if you ask forgiveness, you're smiling in the sun again. Sure this system has a couple cruel loopholes to it. For example, if the Pope accidentally says "Goddammit" when he breaks a plate, and then has a heart attack and dies before confessing his sin, he goes to Hell. No exceptions. Another example: since the fear of sin is so prevalent, Catholics are wary of "doubling up" on sin. So if an unmarried couple decides to fornicate, they can't wear a condom, because then they'd be SINNING TWICE. AT THE SAME TIME.

But for the most part, Catholics have an easy way to sin like crazy and get away with it. If you don't mind doing 'Penance', which is really reciting a bunch of "Hail Mary's". Like I said, repetition is key.

However, I left Catholicism because non-denominational Christianity made more sense. It was more relaxed. And my new preacher managed to take the Bible and apply it to the real world. The real world being why I should vote for Bush or McCain or Reagan's corpse, and not the corrupt Democrat.

So I vote for the guy God endorses, through my preacher. And I count on the facts He gives me. And if the facts aren't exactly in the Bible, I know there's a way to tie it back. What Would Jesus Do? He'd vote Republican. And get rid of the capital gains tax.

CHAPTER 46
Obama: Socialist or Communist?

I have neighbors who emigrated from the Ukraine (they were naturalized... I checked), and I asked them if Obama's presidency reminds them of growing up in Communist USSR. And my neighbor looked me straight in the eye, and said without hesitation, "It's not even close." See, Obama is more of a Communist than anyone in Communist Russia. It's Not. Even. Close.

I left that conversation more afraid than ever.

Now I'm a little too young to remember the Red Scare. But from what I gleaned off my school history books and the way Glenn Beck tells it, the Communist menace was very real, very dangerous, and very big. It was like American Idol.

However, after decades of living with this threat, Ronald Reagan ended Communism by saying. "Tear down this wall, you Russian Guy!" What a hero. When someone asks me if Ronald Reagan deserves a place on Mount Rushmore, I say, "No." I say he deserves the whole damn Mount! Get those other guys off there! Blow their faces off! Or build a mountain on top of the current Mount Rushmore, and put Reagan's face on that.

But now Obama is crapping all over Reagan's spirit by bringing Communism back. Obama has said, and I quote, "I want to spread the wealth and make America a Communist nation. And we're all drinking vodka for breakfast."

Liberals would argue that the previous statement is untrue, and is not an actual quote from Obama. But I have studied all of Obama's speeches, and it turns out that he *has* said, "I want to spread the wealth and make America a Communist nation. And we're all drinking vodka for breakfast." Now he may not have said those words in that particular order, or at the same time. But he has said them. And I just put them together in my own unique way. That is how quotes work.

So we need to stop this Red Menace before it gets out of hand. We must round up all Democrats and interrogate them to the point they confess to being Communist. Then we execute them. In public. Then everyone else will think twice about becoming a Communist.

Now I know the title of this chapter asks if Obama is a socialist or a communist? To me the words are really quite interchangeable. I think they mean practically the same thing, so they're equally bad. No need doing a Google search to find out for sure.

Besides, we're not a nation of socialists, spreading the wealth around. Now liberals will argue that the fire department, the armed forces, education, and police are examples of things we all pay for, but which we might not all need. So technically, that is socialism.

Well, I can't deny that. But what I can do is make sure I use those services. So once a year I start a fire (not in my house... that would be silly) in my backyard, or in the woods behind my house, so the fire department comes to put it out. That way I know I got my money's worth. Same for police. I call 911 every week, saying an intruder is in my house. When the cops get there I say I scared him off. They act disappointed, but they should be relieved, knowing they're needed and that they didn't have to get in a dangerous gunfight with an intruder. Yet they never thank me. In fact, they seem angry all the time.

But deep down, I know they're thankful we're not Communists.

CHAPTER 47
The Debt.
15 trillion reasons why Obama is stupid

As a Christian who believes the Rapture will happen any day now (please please, let it happen on my watch!), I think it's ludicrous to bother spending money on environmental measures that might help cool the planet, stabilize the climate, and keep us from making the world inhospitable to humans. Why waste money preventing something that won't happen in 50 years, when the Rapture's going to happen first? See, we won't need Earth then.

But we must reduce our debt for the sake of our grandchildren, so they're not saddled with it 50 years from now!

Amazingly enough, my threshold for the debt being too high was when stupid poopy pants Obama took over as president. Sure the debt reached a trillion bucks under Reagan, and climbed under Bush 1 and Bush 2, and even some with Clinton. But those numbers and all the zeroes didn't really seem that big until Obama was inaugurated. How about that? Perspectives *can* change. It just goes to show: things aren't a big deal until Obama does it. The flag lapel pin? Not a big deal until Obama didn't wear one. Placing your hand on your heart for the National Anthem? Not a big deal until Obama didn't do it. Having a growing debt that reaches into the trillions? Once again, it's a big deal now. That's the kind of power Obama wields, and it's why we must stop him. You may call it convoluted. I call it unconvoluted.

Meanwhile, Obama likes to throw the blame around for the ever-increasing debt. His litany is a broken record: Not enough tax revenues coming in because so many people are out of work. The wars. Paying out more unemployment benefits. Paying more in food stamps and welfare because the recession put so many more people into poverty. Hey, those people chose to get laid off! They didn't work hard enough!

Either way, we know the truth. Obama is lying. The truth is, as John Boehner and Eric Cantor and Mitch McConnell have so eloquently stated: "Obama has been on a spending spree." That's right. He's just being wasteful, spending all that money. On stuff. Which is why we need to cut spending on Medicare, Medicaid, Social Security and social programs and wasteful government jobs. Since I don't really know what the people with government jobs actually do, I can only assume their jobs are wasteful. But if they do serve some sort of purpose, then we must ask them to sacrifice for the greater good. Sometimes our leaders need to make what they call the "tough decisions." And those decisions are the toughest on those schmucks who voted for the other guy.

But the bigger problem is this: Because Obama wasted money on frivolous things (I can't name those right now off the top of my head), we need to make big cuts in the "essentials" like Medicare, Social Security, Education... that sort of thing. Makes sense, right?

Cut spending, we cut debt. It's not a difficult concept. So don't try to make it complicated. But that's what liberals do. They always try to muddy things up with *details*. But guess what, liberals? No one wants to hear all that. Big problems have simple solutions. Everyone knows that.

The debt is a big problem. So cut spending! Simple.

Problem solved in three words. (Two words if I didn't add the "so" at the beginning.). Liberals, meanwhile, try to point out that cutting spending actually hurts the economy, because our overall spending power is reduced. For example, you lay off a few thousand federal workers, then they don't have as much money to spend back into the economy, and the engine of capitalism suddenly lacks the grease it needs to move along. And it makes it even harder to pay down the debt.

But get a load of the liberal solution: spend MORE now to get the economy going again, and THEN make cuts later. Yeah, right, fool me once, you won't get fooled again! Liberals won't stop spending. They're addicted to it. And they just want their next fix, turning their House upside down, looking for something, *anything* to spend money on. Underground solar panels. Aircraft carriers in Kansas. Education for 4-year olds.

Sorry, liberals. It's time to detox. No more spending. Time to try the conservative method *for once.* Choke off the funds, pay down the debt, and THEN we'll get to jumpstarting the economy again. Because now, more than ever, the debt is the biggest problem we face. And it must be a really big biggest problem, because it's been Number 1 with us conservatives for almost a year. Health care, illegals, jobs, taxes, Obama's birth certificate... all those held the top spot for a few months at a time the last few years. But on the debt, we're deadly serious. Until gas prices get really high.

CHAPTER 48
Having premarital sex is worse than having cancer

One thing that bothers me a lot, even though I don't know much about it, is the HPV vaccine. Apparently, Obama's all for it, which is my number one concern. But also, HPV sounds a lot like HIV, which is scary stuff. So right there, my "this is bad news" radar is going off like Spiderman's spidersense. HIV is a death sentence, except for athletes. And from what I read in the papers and on the Internet (mostly the Internet), the HPV vaccine just makes teenage girls want to have sex. It's giving them permission to "do it." Which would have been great for me back when I was a teenager. But now, it's just wrong.

Now I'm no doctor, or a teenage girl, but I'm pretty sure I know what I'm talking about here. It all breaks down like this: The HPV vaccine helps prevent against types of cervical cancer, which is something you can get from sex. So this vaccine is a license for girls to have sex. Go for it, girls! Now nothing bad can happen to you from having sex. Way to go, doctors!

Don't these liberals realize that we need to scare teenage girls from having sex? If they don't have the fear, then they'll have the sex. And let me remark on the elephant in the room: maybe these women deserve the cancer they get. They were warned! "You wanna bang? You gonna die." Seems like it's not a lot to ask girls to not have sex. I did it for 28 years! And I'm a guy! It's harder for guys to not have sex than girls... that's a scientific fact.

Now if one caught cervical cancer by means other than sex, I'd be all for the vaccine. Heck, I'd even take it.

But sometimes teaching fear of sex isn't enough for our young people. They must be taught abstinence. In school. And the best way to do that is to show graphic images of STDs every day from kindergarten through college. And then have morning prayer.

But Obama's idea of sex ed is to give kindergartners porn and have Jenna Jameson as the teacher. So forgive me for objecting to this, and for wanting a country where we're not all a bunch of sex maniacs. Forgive me for wanting to live in a country without Internet porn. Forgive me for wanting a country where only married couples screw each other's brains out, as God intended. I guess I'm just old-fashioned.

One last postscript: If we teach abstinence, people will stay married longer. Now I'm not saying they'll live longer. But more couples will get married as soon as they turn 18 (or whatever the age of consent is in their state... Pennsylvania's is 16, FYI). Those couples, who have waited until they had a marriage bed for sex, will be rewarded for their long wait. And get a much longer marriage out of it. Instead of spending college years and their 20s bed-hopping, they can get a jump-start on marriage, maturing together, having that first sip of alcohol as the kids play outside, and looking forward to a potential seven decades of wedded bliss.

CHAPTER 49
The Tea Party: A step in the right direction

Yes it is.

The Tea Party represents about 25% to 30% of the population, give or take. But with our primary election process, that 25% can influence and control the way we govern. And that, my friends, is Democracy.

The Tea Party is an example of a natural, organically-grown, grassroots movement complete with pre-printed signs, the support of Fox News, regular e-mail alerts, a variety of avenues to donate, and the backing of a few well-connected billionaires. Yet with so many factors working against the Tea Party, they became a powerful force of good.

Because of them our politicians in Washington are cutting budgets. Because of them we have the lowest tax rates ever. Because of them we took back the House of Representatives. Because of them we've nearly had THREE government shutdowns in less than a year! That's gotta be some sort of record!

But this is just the beginning. The Tea Party can't be satisfied with being the most powerful force in the world. Complacency leads to downfall. Greed leads to growth.

And their tactics need to be tweaked as well. By that I mean: GET MEAN! The time for civil discourse is over. The Tea Party has been talking for three years now. It's time to take it up a notch and stop being so nice. Those signs that compared Obama to Hitler might have played well in 2010, but these days, we need more. Like Photoshopped images of Obama pooping on schoolchildren. Like a contingent of Tea Party members devoting no less than 12 hours a day adding their two cents in the comments section of news stories, from ABCNew.com to Yahoo. And those comments better be condescending and loaded with anger and in ALL CAPS. Because if we can't say anything mean about Obama, then don't say anything at all.

And also, buy Glenn Beck's books. From spy novels to political essays to Christmas Sweaters to historical accounts, that guy can write anything! Why his works aren't required reading in schools is beyond me. And in between all this writing, hosting a TV and radio show, being a family man and traveling the country hosting rallies, he still found time to help launch the Tea Party and make it what it is today.
The Tea Party. You're all invited. But chances are, they won't like you.

CHAPTER 50
I don't have a problem with adulterers preaching abstinence

I'm back to talking about abstinence again. Talking about it is one thing I can't "abstain" from. HA!

The decision to have sex is a very important one. You don't want to have sex too early or too often and be called a slut (if you're a girl). And you don't want to wait too long and be called a loser (if you're a guy.). Also you'd probably want to be in love first.

Fortunately, marriage takes that guesswork out of the equation. You get married, you have sex for the first time that night, and it's all easy-peasy Japaneasy. There's no awkwardness, no seedy hotel rooms, no embarrassment about buying condoms. It's all amazing and you will both climax simultaneously, just like in the movies.

However, a majority of people don't wait until marriage to have sex. It's like they're animals programmed to want sex, as if it serves some sort of purpose, like to keep the species going. Which is just nonsense.

Movies and TV and music and Internet and magazines and books and gossip are loaded with sex, so it's no wonder that so many people want to have sex. It didn't used to be this way. Back in Puritanical times, NO ONE wanted to have sex. Sex was dirty. It was shameful. It was punished with jagged castrations and genital mutilations. It was awesome.

But now, you see sex everywhere. And it's just too difficult for the average unmarried human being to resist the temptation of sex. Which is why we need the government to help out. Because so many of our young people respect politicians, we need them to preach abstinence. Our sex lives are too personal to be handled on our own.

Now I'm not naïve. I know that most politicians (the Democrats) weren't virgins when they got married. They banged each other at Woodstock and haven't stopped since. (Thanks for all the herpes, Democrats!) Share an elevator with a Democrat and have his child nine months later. So the Democrats can't be trusted on this one. But the conservatives? We can trust them. Just look at 'em! Do you really think Mitch McConnell had sex before he was married? Or Chris Christie? Or Sarah Palin? No freakin' way! They were virgins until their wedding nights.

Now you may scoff at this notion. You may say, "I don't think that's true. I'm Glen Rice."

But on the off chance a Republican had sex before he or she was married (I guess anything's possible), then I'm sure the next morning they hurried to church and became "born-again virgins". Yep, that's a real thing. It's like a do-over for virginity. You get one per lifetime. Use it or lose it.

But I find it highly dubious that our conservative people in Congress did have sex before marriage. If they had, why do they talk so much about the importance of abstinence? They know that it would be RIDICULOUS if they didn't also practice what they preach! That would make them hypocrites. And if there's one thing a politician won't accept, it's being labeled a hypocrite (unless he's a Democrat. Then it's a requirement.)

Now the elephant in the room on this topic is Newt Gingrich. Rumors abound (never proven) that he committed adultery on his first two wives. Even if that were true, he didn't cast aside his mistresses like old cheese. He married them. So give the guy credit. He's got an eye toward the future.

It was Newt who proudly proclaimed the Republicans stood for "Family Values". While that term was flexible enough to mean what we wanted it to mean (no gayness, sex only in the bounds of marriage, a great deal at Walmart), it also hamstrung politicians like Gingrich, whom the ladies all loved. So Newt, in his wisdom, found a way to compromise without compromising his beliefs.

By marrying his mistresses and sexually satisfying the lucky ladies who couldn't get enough of his charm and that devilish grin, he was able to create more "families." So in a sense, he's three times the man the rest of us are!

So when Newt preaches (or at least hints at) abstinence as part of a family values platform, you know you can trust him. He's a family man. He's a family man. He's a family man.

CHAPTER 51
We must take our country back!
From something.

"We must take our country back!"

If there is a lull in the rally, or if it's starting to rain, or you just want to get people to yell and cheer, that's all you have to say.

"We must take our country back!"

Plus it doesn't sound that distorted when yelled through a bullhorn.

"We must take our country back!"

It's the ultimate catchphrase. It says everything, without saying anything at all.

It works because no one likes it when things are taken from them. I worked with a guy who took my lunch one day. Pissed me off. So I poured sugar in his gas tank. And made threatening phone calls to his children. Now we're even. (Full disclosure... I'd forgotten my lunch that day.)

But the point was, having a lunch stolen from me was enough to get me all riled up. So imagine my reaction when someone takes my country from me. I don't love anything more than my country. So I will do whatever it takes to get it back.

That's why I, and millions like me, want to take the country back from the people who took it from us in the first place. Obama and his dumbass supporters. They took it back first. And now we aim to take it back again.

Because a nation isn't to be shared. It's to be taken. Back.

Liberals, however are like toddlers. They want things to be fair, so we all share things like commies in Cuba. Guess what, you Obama-lovers! Life isn't fair. It's not some "This land is my land, this land is your land" claptrap. This land is my land, end of story. I'll let you live here as long as you share my opinions.

CHAPTER 52
Child labor works for me

Kids are lazy.

They didn't use to be. Back in the good old days (c. 1900), kids worked for their meals and brought home a few nickels to help the family. It was a magical time. Kids were lovable scamps calling "Extra Extra! Read all about it!" while holding up today's edition. Or they were lovable orphans singing songs. Or little rascals. Or nefarious pickpockets who were rightly put to death when captured. Either way, the system of child labor worked.

Then what happened? The Labor Movement happened. When workers weren't going on strike for every damn little thing ("We want a living wage! We don't want to work on Christmas Day! My arm won't stop bleeding where the machine cut it off!"), they were complaining about their jobs. Whiners. Work is to be loved.

133

Work kept the kids off the streets. Unless the streets is where they worked. But over the last 100 years, more kids have left the workforce. And that's been a sad state of affairs.

I say we need to put kids back to work. Once they're old enough to walk and talk, they're old enough to bring home a paycheck (or at least intern for free... because you can't put a price on experience). And like I said in my enlightening chapter on education, kids will work for a much smaller paycheck, which is better for a business's profit margin. How inspiring is that?

Kids can readily do many dangerous jobs. First and foremost among them is coal-mining.

It makes perfect sense. For one thing, did you know another name for child is minor? I found that out the hard way, and we'll leave it at that. So they're called "Minors" for a reason. Not because they're under 18, but because they should work in mines!

Besides being able to fit into tight spaces and scoot along the tunnels, I think a kid would love to be a coalminer. Go to a Chuckie Cheese sometime. Watch how those kids scurry about in those plastic tubes. They're having fun! In fact, a smart management team could make a game of it, and reward the children not with boring old paychecks, but with spider rings and taffy bars. Just give the kids some tickets throughout the day, and they can redeem them at the front desk when they clock out. "Do you want to redeem your points now or save them for the AM/FM clock radio?"

And if caught in a mine, they can survive longer, because they need less air and food to survive. And the holes we drill so they can escape don't have to be as wide.

Putting kids to work means we have to worry less about outsourcing jobs to India and China. No longer will we compete with a foreign nation's efficient payment system (70¢ per day), because our kids will work cheap at just about any job.

And studies show that kids are better learners than adults. A 2-year-old's capacity for learning is 10 times that of a 32-year-old. So upon birth, we start training kids for their careers, which they'll take up by the time they're eight. Each kid will be randomly assigned an occupation, and the training will commence.

Now we'll need to make some adjustments. Cockpits of commercial airliners will need to be retrofitted to handle the shorter legs and arms. Surgical tables will need to be lowered. We'll need lighter-weight guns for kid cops. Premium liquor must be moved to the bottom shelf for easier reach for our "kid-tenders".

There is an exception. Stripping and exotic dancing will still be done by barely legal teenagers. Because children shouldn't be exploited.

CHAPTER 53
Balanced Budget Amendment.
If it sounds good, it must BE GOOD.

There are some wonderful words in the English language. Harmony. Chimes. Lullaby. Credit deferred swap. But my new favorite is Balanced Budget Amendment. It is the Dream Team of a phrase, so perfect in the way it sounds and what it represents. No one could possibly argue against, or badmouth it in any way.

Unless your name is Barack Obama.

The Balanced Budget Amendment is exactly what its name implies: a rule that prohibits Congress from spending more money than it takes in. Essentially we ask that the government not spend money like drunken sailors (I had no idea that when sailors got drunk they love to shop, but who am I to argue against a popular metaphor?). Instead they must be reined in and spend money like your average household.

In my house we don't spend any more than we take in. Except for the home loan, of course. We couldn't pay all that off at once. And the kids' college. And the cars. And the months where our credit card bill is a little higher (Christmas, car repairs, the day I discovered Amazon.com). But for everything else, our family does not spend more than it takes in. And government needs to be the same way.

And conservatives have made the first big step: creating a bill with a great name. Republicans are FANTASTIC at semantics. They know that in these fast-paced times, there is little time for explanation. However, the population is smart enough to figure out the explanation from just a few words. "Balanced Budge Amendment" is a prime example. No explanation necessary.

And the time you save on explanations can be used to tear down liberal ideas and people. "The Balanced Budget Amendment just makes sense. Casey Anthony is sleeping in Barney Frank's guest house."

Republicans play with words like Larry Bird shoots three-pointers. Awesomely. Here are some examples:
Millionaires aren't "rich". They're "job creators."
Bush isn't "stupid." He's a "real person."
Liberals don't "invest". They "tax & spend."
Republicans don't oppose "gay marriage". They want to "protect marriage."
Liberals aren't "pro-choice." They're "pro-abortion" or "psycho baby killers"

The words we choose are important. Because while the substance of a law, idea or proposal may be good, it's the title that truly defines it. For example, if the "Balanced Budget Amendment" was called "A Financial Catastrophe Just Waiting to Happen," it wouldn't be as popular.

Words matter. That's why I'm changing my name to Mr. Awesome. Because I want to be awesome. And it's why my friend Jimmy changed his name to "Anonymous" in an effort to collect royalties from certain works of art, poetry, music and literature.

CHAPTER 54
Michael Moore is fat.
Rush Limbaugh is just extra full of great ideas.

One of my liberal neighbors was going on and on about how

capitalism is bad, how our health care system is broken, and how the pretense for the war in Iraq was based on lies. He talked for about an hour. I asked him where he got this information. And he rattled off a few of the usual sources: New York Times, Washington Post, Mother Jones. And then he mentioned Michael Moore. That's when I knew I had him and the argument was mine. I pointed out that Michael Moore is fat.

Game. Set. Match.

Michael Moore is not just fat. He also looks like he smells. And he wears glasses, and he's got a wimpy, nasally voice, and he has real trouble properly framing a shot. But I don't see him as much of a threat to our movement. Because he only makes a movie every three years or so. That's like, six hours in 10 years. Not a lot of time to get his message out. And since conservatives will never watch his movies, but still complain loudly about them, Michael Moore's effect on policy change is about as nonexistent as celery on his plate.

Meanwhile, Rush Limbaugh (from here-on referred to as RUSH), is on the air for at least four hours EVERY DAY. That's 20 hours per week, almost 100 hours a month, 1,200 hours a year, on one of the most cutting-edge media outlets of our time. Daytime Radio.

So while Michael Moore spends years filming and editing his movies to get his message just right (snicker), RUSH is on the air LIVE every day, ready to take down any obnoxious caller who disagrees with him (damn you, screener!), while also working without a script for the whole show. Now while I don't think he's perfect, he's as close as they come. And he's been doing this for so long, he's definitely earned his place on the Mount Rushmore of Conservative Voices. And also on the real Mount Rushmore.

Rush was a conservative pundit before it became cool. He taught all the up and comers that you didn't have to watch what you say out of fear of retribution from the left. You could say any racist, homophobic, sexist thing you wanted. And your audience WOULD NOT CARE! In fact, they'd like you all the more for it... *because you're telling it like it is*. RUSH never worried about being politically correct. Conservatives hate political correctness, because it makes it against the rules to say the "n-word."

Then RUSH discovered you didn't even have to tell the truth (as the "mainstream media" saw it), because his audience wouldn't even fact-check him. Why? Because to the audience, what RUSH said was the truth! And no amount of liberal media or "rational" explanation was going to sway them. If RUSH says almost $800 billion of Obama's stimulus money went to infrastructure projects (RUSH did say this), then it must be true. At least to those of us who listen. I mean, why go from one media outlet to another to figure out the truth for ourselves, when we can just listen to RUSH and be done with it? Even if what he says isn't technically true, so what? More people believe him instead of the facts. Which makes what he says more believable in my opinion. It's simple logic.

So what RUSH says is the truth, a source of info we can pass on to our friends. Unless he calls someone a "slut" or "prostitute." Then he's just being an entertainer.

I think it's terrible the way liberals mock RUSH'S weight. Like he's the only guy with a weight problem. Maybe he's got a slow metabolism, OK? Cut the guy some slack. But what's even worse... liberals claim Rush is gay. Oh, really? Would a gay man get married FOUR TIMES to female adults? That's right, RUSH respects the sanctity of marriage that much.

But because the greatest minds always get the most abuse, liberals don't stop with the "RUSH is our punching bag" attitude. They mocked his painkiller addiction! That's sickening! Addiction is a disease, especially when it affects rich, white guys. Show some compassion! Rush would show you the same respect if *you* were addicted to prescription medication. However, RUSH is correct to point out that being unable to stop doing crack, cocaine, heroin, meth, and marijuana is a weakness that a decades-long stint in the penitentiary can fix.

Now I feel I must point out the elephant in the room. Because if we're being honest (and this is an honest, nothing-held-back book) we must address the rumor that RUSH was caught with dozens of Viagra pills on his way back from a trip to the Dominican Republic. Liberals made a big deal about this, and some of them actually gleefully state that RUSH was at the DR to have sex with 10-year-old boys. That is sickening (not the sodomy charge, but the fact that liberals would make it. Is there nothing they won't do to bring down a family man like RUSH?). It's obvious that liberals didn't consider any of these explanations:

• RUSH was bringing the Viagra home for his buddies who can't get it up like he does. Because RUSH is a damn stallion. Giddyup!

• RUSH took the pills with him just in case he got laid by such a long string of Dominican hotties that he might, for the first time ever, get a little tired. But it turns out he never needed the pills. So he never unpacked them.

• RUSH accidentally picked up Al Gore's bag at the hotel before leaving for the airport.

• RUSH was never at the DR. It was a dream collectively implanted on the total population, like "Inception" on steroids. See, it was all a dream! And we just mixed up RUSH with Leonardo DiCaprio. Honest mistake on our part.

• They were just Tic Tacs. RUSH keeps his breath minty fresh. Because he never knows what the day will bring. Maybe a wedding. His.

• These aren't the drugs you're looking for. Move along.

RUSH is also very rich. Like super-duper rich. So he really understands the burden rich people face in this country. He's one of the few who knows firsthand how higher marginal tax rates can cripple those in our nation who are successful. (And money always equals success. If you ain't rich, you're a loser. Dig a hole and crawl in.).

Meanwhile, he never loses sight of the plight of the middle class, that group of people who never worked as hard as he did. In fact, legions of his fans don't even make $100,000/year. Yet RUSH doesn't admonish them for their lack of success. If anything, he gives them the tools to work harder. Tools like easy-to-remember soundbites that can be reposted on message boards and comments sections all over the country. So while these people may not have the skills or the drive or the talent RUSH has, he still lowers himself to inspire these people and spread his word. He truly is a hero.

Also, he came up with the term "Halfrican."

CHAPTER 55
Do I like politicians who talk like me? You betcha!

I want a president I'd like to have a beer with. Not some Ivy League-educated snotnose that spouts off crazy math formulas or 50-cent words like "fiscal" and "fiduciary" and "parliamentary." I want a president I can understand, not some guy who happened to buy Word-of-the-Day toilet paper.

And Obama? He's one of those smug fancy-talking prima donnas. He's their king. Their dictator. Their... well I don't have another word, which goes to prove I'm no walking thesaurus. I'm a plain-spoken folk just like you.

Like a lot of people, I can't understand most of what Obama says. Even after he says, "Let me be clear..." he still doesn't make much sense. It's like he's mocking us, pretending to clarify his endless stream of bullshit when he's really just babbling on incoherently. "Let me be clear. The stimulus will put people to work immediately, and help families across America." Whoa, slow down Professor Know-it-All. I need details. Some charts. Something that fits on a bumper sticker and which includes the phrase "Obama sucks."

That's why I really got to hand it to Rep. Joe Wilson. Because when he shouted "You Lie!" to Obama during a speech to Congress, it showed me that Joe Wilson has class, courage, and he could understand what the hell Obama was talking about. I bet if it had been Obama talking back to his own self during that speech, he wouldn't have been so plain-spoken as Joe. He would have said, "You speak not the truth to this audience that seats as one before you!" I swear, it seems like Obama talks like a high school kid writing an essay. He's just filling up space with words.

That's why Ronald Reagan, George W. Bush and Sarah Palin are so popular. They talk like real people. They don't talk down to their audience. They include lots of uh's, and um's, and "I'll get back to you on that's". One truly gets the sense they are no smarter than the rest of us. And that makes me feel good, because I don't like feeling dumb.

Case in point: When Sarah Palin debated Joe Biden in 2008, she revolutionized the whole debate process within 60 seconds. Normally these debates were stuffy affairs with no personality. They were BORING. But Sarah immediately let loose, winking at the camera, saying "You betcha," and wearing a dress. It totally threw Joe ("Can I call you Joe") off his game. And she showed the world that she is like us... a regular Mom who was also governor, has a wardrobe expense account, her very own bus and millions in a bank account without having a real job.

However, this is not to say I want a leader that's not brilliant. I do. I just don't want him to make a big show of his brilliance. He should keep that to himself. He should know everything about everything, but also come across as someone no smarter than me. And have a 200 bowling average. And be able to ride a horse. And pilot a plane. And raise a family. And eat a corn dog without looking weird on camera.

Essentially, be perfect, but don't come across as someone who's perfect.

CHAPTER 56
I'm a Single Issue Voter. On these 10 Issues.

The following issues are all dealbreakers for me. If you disagree with me at all on any of these issues, you don't get my vote. It's just that simple.

1. Abortion

2. The Designated Hitter

3. The awesomeness of Hank Williams Jr.

4. Unions: They suck

5, That Kourtney Kardashian is the cutest one.

6. The most important meal of the day: Breakfast.

7. No statehood for Guam

8. English should be the only language spoken in the United States

9. NASCAR Rules!

   10. Your lucky number must be 472.

CHAPTER 57
An Objective Look at the Founding Fathers:
The Greatest People Ever Times a Million

I love, love, love the Founding Fathers. Because they founded this great country of ours, wrote the Constitution, and invented bifocals.

I also love them because no matter what liberal lies a liberal liar throws at you, all you have to say is, 'That's not what the Founding Fathers wanted." It's amazing how that shuts them up. Or you can spring the whole "That's totally unconstitutional" on them. By making big pronouncements like that, you can make a liberal feel small and insignificant. Take this exchange I had with some liberal loser on a comments page about a Yahoo News article on a shortage of qualified schoolbus drivers:

Mikelaw4564789 (That's me): Maybe if we had more prayer in school, these bus drivers would get back to work.

Smithers 212: I'm not sure how prayer in school would create the funds needed to attract skilled bus drivers.

Mikelaw4564789: You stupid liberal. The kids could pray for bus drivers.

Smithers 212: I'm not a liberal, and it's not nice to call someone stupid. I think school prayer is another topic altogether.

Mikelaw4564789: Schools would be better with prayer. That's a fact! It's what the Founding Fathers wanted.

Smithers 212: No, the Founding Fathers never endorsed prayer in schools.

Mikelaw4564789: It's in the Constitution!

Smithers 212: Actually, the Constitution states that Freedom of Religion is also freedom from religion, hence separation of church and state.

Mikelaw4564789: I'm not talking about states. I'm talking about SCHOOLS, you dumba$$.

Smithers 212: I just can't argue with you. Have a nice life.

See there? Victory. I gave him the Founding Fathers/Constitution one-two combo, and he went down like Apollo Creed in "Rocky IV."

Liberals hate the Founding Fathers. And the Constitution. And the American Flag. Of course they deny this, but that just convinces me even more. Because liberals only lie. So if they actually said, "I hate the Constitution. It sucks." I would assume they love it. I dare Obama to say THAT. Go on, Mr. President, say you hate the Constitution. I promise to not believe you or make a big deal about it.

I think liberals (and Obama!) hate the Founding Fathers because it makes them feel insecure about their own lives. Their own existence of playing hacky sack all day and being a barista at Starbucks pales in comparison to FOUNDING the GREATEST COUNTRY ON EARTH! So a little jealousy creeps in. They're projecting their own shortcomings onto the Founding Fathers. And the Founding Fathers aren't around to protect themselves. Because they're dead. Sounds to me like liberals have "Daddy issues." Founding Daddies Issues.

So it's up to us conservatives to defend their honor and legacy and point out that everything the Founding Fathers stood for and accomplished is perfect. They're like saints, only better.

143

In fact, the Founding Fathers were so awesome that many of them because president of the United States. George Washington, John Adams, Thomas Jefferson, and John Quincy Adams (who was the youngest Founding Father as a 9-year-old). That shows you how great they are. No other group created as many presidents (except maybe the Skull & Bones). So right there the Founding Fathers have the ultimate résumé booster. POTUS. Once you put that on your résumé, you can pretty much get any job you want. "Well, your internship at Lehman Brothers is impressive, as is your time as President of the United States. I think we can find a place for you here at Best Buy. Do you know much about digital cameras?"

Now liberals hate George Washington because he never told a lie, so he's not like them. Sure, the cherry tree story about his honesty is in fact a fabrication. The true story is that Washington murdered a local whore named Cherry Tree with an axe, and told everybody about it. Every little gruesome detail. That, my friends, is real honesty. Of course we couldn't tell that story to children, so "Cherry Tree" became "cherry tree". And "chopped her body into pieces and ate the flesh" became "chopped down".

In fact, George Washington (The original George W) was so honest that he would tell his wife she looked fat in those bloomers, even if she didn't ask! Ballsy and truthful. So when liberals lie (every time they open their mouths), it's an affront to the honesty of George Washington. It's like telling our first president to go to Hell.

Now liberals like to point out that Thomas Jefferson knocked up one of his slaves. But if you look at the history (or let a historian like Glenn Beck or Michele Bachmann tell it to you), he did it for the good of the country while on the pursuit of happiness. Plus it was his way of showing the slaves that he would treat them right. All night. Boom chak-a-waka.

So whenever you have a problem, just ask, "What would the Founding Fathers do?" Unless it's a problem with your iPad. Because the Founding Fathers didn't have those.

CHAPTER 58
The world will implode if we let two dudes get married.

I can sum up my objections to gay marriage in two words: Ewww. Gross.

But a lot of liberals don't take that as a serious argument. Fortunately, there's someone else who's against gay marriage. God. And His Son Jesus. So that about settles it, don't it? I got God on my side. All they have is some ridiculous theory that a lifelong commitment to someone you love be recognized by all and symbolized by marriage not be infringed upon just because that person you love is the same sex. Yeah, let's see that fly in the Real World. God said no to gay marriage, and that's that.

Well, actually, he said that it's an abomination for a man to lie with another man. It's in Leviticus. Or Deuteronomy. One of the early books of the Bible. Either way, it's absolute and NOT open for interpretation. "Lie" means "lie." Which in this case means "have sex with". In the biblical sense it DOES NOT mean a fib or untruth. (However, when Obama and Biden stand up there and say Obamacare won't destroy our country, you could say they are "lying together." But it's not in the biblical sense. Though what they do after hours is their business. And ours.).

Now why doesn't it just say "sex" in the Bible? Simple. Sex is a dirty word, and the Bible is a clean book. It has to be rated PG, for all audiences. That's why all the adultery, executions, child murders, famine, plagues, pestilence, crucifixions (both upside down and rightside up), incest and genocidal flooding in the Bible are all described in subtle, tasteful ways. It's like what that company in Utah does to DVDs like "Die Hard", editing them so no one will see the sex and violence or hear the dirty language. Also, "Die Hard" is now called "Bruce Willis Action Movie". Because "Die" is a bad word, and "Hard" can be construed as something off-color. (Here's a hint: erect penis). Also the edited version is 5 minutes long... it ends after John McClain gets off the plane in the opening scene.

So a man can't lie with a man. And if he can't even lie with him, then he certainly can't marry him. Not unless they're going to be in separate beds. Which in marriage is ludicrous.

Besides, marriage isn't just about "love". It's also about making babies. Keeping the species going. It's about having just enough sex to make a couple babies and that's it. And if you happen to find a mate who shares enough of your taste in television shows and isn't completely turned off by your Hummel collection, then you have a rock-solid foundation to have a long-lasting, routine-based, tolerable marriage.

Now some would contend that if procreation is the main reason to be married, then you might as well divorce once the kids are made. Well, it turns out it's not that simple. After the kids are born, you must raise them. However, some say that once the kids are out of the house, you can get divorced then. NOT SO!

Because you need to provide a home for your kids to come home to, in case their job is outsourced (Thanks, Obama!) or if they end up pregnant at the hands of their Eastern Linguistics professor (Thanks, Liberal Arts Institution!), or if they're too lazy to get a job after six years of college because they think they'll be famous for being themselves (Thanks, every show on Disney Channel!). So when they must come home, you must be a married couple when they get there. Otherwise the kids will be traumatized. Or worse, blame your divorce for their own shortcomings.

Now being a man/woman couple, as we all know, is the best way to raise kids. I don't think anyone can argue with that. You might as well argue the existence of the sun. But even with a solid man/woman base of support, nurturing and discipline, some kids can lose their way. For example, if your teenager becomes addicted to drugs or alcohol, then it wasn't your fault. In our world today, shaped by the likes of Obama and his free-love-let's-all-smoke-crack crowd, the new rules and norms of society have placed a tremendous burden on our kids. If they try to do the right thing, they're met with ridicule and giggles. I know this, because I've seen clips of Gossip Girl. Alcohol and drug addiction is a disease. A sickness. And you can't be blamed for that. And no one can blame you for trying to get them help.

If a child of a gay couple becomes addicted to drugs or alcohol, it's because his parents are gay.

But back to the Bible and my chapter title. Now the Bible speaks often of end times, and my church speaks often of it as well. Because they know what their audience wants to hear! Enough with all that talk about loving thy neighbor. Get to the Apocalypse! Scare us so we'll vote Republican!

The book of Revelation states clearly how the world will end. Unfortunately, I can't make any sense of it. I wonder if John ate the wrong kind of mushrooms before he wrote it. Fortunately, my former preacher (embezzlement charges landed him in a prison known as a Baptist church) spent all of 1999 analyzing the book of Revelation, chapter by chapter for those of us in his congregation. Those sermons, in addition to watching "The Seventh Sign" on my own (independent study) helped me understand the Apocalypse a whole lot better.

But perhaps my former preacher was wrong when he said the Book of Revelation foretold that the end of the world would happen in the year 2000. But like he had a logical explanation for this: "God gave us a four-year reprieve after the result of the 2000 election." True story. What wasn't true is that the preacher gave us our life savings (which is WORTHLESS in heaven) back. "That money is with God now."

However, one added lesson from all that was that just about anything can bring about the end of the world. We don't know when it will happen, but God has shown how he can -- and I want to be delicate here because He's watching -- fly off the handle like Joe Pesci in "Goodfellas." One snap of His holy fingers and we're all blind. And dead.

So when He calls being gay an abomination, and when He calls marriage a most sacred union, you can see what might happen when we mix the two together. Gay Marriage. Yikes. That's like barfing in His salad. God may decide we just aren't worth the trouble anymore. As soon as two guys say "I do," God may decide to say, "I won't."

And Obama, well, he once claimed to be against gay marriage. But that's something Democrats running for president *just say*. Like when we tell children that they can be anything they want to be when they grow up. Or when as teenagers we tell a girl, "I love you." Deep down we know how we really feel. And what we're hoping to get out of it: Ahead in this world.

So Obama isn't just lying, he also supports the destruction of our world. Thanks, Mr. President. Why not just push the Button now and save us all some time? There's enough out there to piss God off, so why bother with the gay marriage thing? Let. It. Go. So gay people can't get married. What's the big deal? They're still allowed to drive, to eat in restaurants, and live together. A marriage certificate is just a piece of paper. Don't fall on your sword for that. And when death do you part, just know you'll wake up in Hell.

CHAPTER 59
Tax cuts cured my impotence

Tax cuts can do damn near anything. That's what Jesus said. In fact, inventing the tax cut was one of His first miracles. It's in the book of Luke. It's real subtle, but it's there. Find the right biblical scholar, and he'll explain it to you.

There are a few absolutes in life. A cat will land feet first. Dr. House will be wrong four times before getting it right. Jogging the morning after eating Chipotle is a terrible, gut-splitting idea.

And tax cuts create jobs. Like magic. It's amazing how Obama just doesn't seem to "get this." I've heard thousands of times how tax cuts create jobs, and how tax increases destroy them. And the more something is said, the more likely it's the truth. It's not rocket science. If it was, a tax increase would just put that rocket scientist out of work.

I just don't understand how Obama refuses to listen to something that's so logical. If a business owner doesn't have to pay taxes, he can use that money saved to hire people. Sounds like a great deal to me. Then the money goes to a happy new employee, and not the government. And studies show (I'm not sure which studies, but I'm sure the Heritage Foundation could create one) that business owners always spend whatever extra money they have hiring new employees. This way they don't burden their current employees with extra work. Why have 10 people do the work of 10 people, when an employer can have 20 people do the work of 10? Everyone wins! Or the employer can keep the 10 workers, and give them all big raises with his tax cut money. Everyone wins again! Or the business owner can keep it for himself and create jobs for yacht-builders.

Liberals say this way of economic thinking is bullshit. Because they don't think too highly of business owners and CEOs. It's all jealousy on their part. If they were CEOs, they wouldn't complain. But because they're really just unemployed layabouts waiting for their government check while watching Jerry Springer on their big-screen TVs, they want to blame someone for their troubles. And the CEOs are an easy target. Because who looks out for them? American CEOs are the forgotten people, like child diamond miners in Sierra Leone.

Tax cuts can cure the common cold.

Sounds crazy? It's not. Tax cuts are the basis of all good things. Tax cuts mean more money in the hand for everyone. And studies show (Heritage Foundation again) that happier people don't get sick as often. More happy = less illness = fewer germs. And suddenly the common cold is a thing of the past, because we're all so happy from our tax cuts.

Now Bush II gave us the biggest tax cuts of all time. And no one can argue the 2000s weren't awesome. Go to any country club and the members there will tell you how wonderful it was. If they'll let you in.

And the best thing is, we still have so many more taxes to cut! We can keep slicing and dicing tax rates until they reach zero! If some tax cuts are good, bigger tax cuts must be great. It's like ice cream!

But liberals don't like ice cream. They want us to eat okra dipped in pig vomit. They want taxes raised, especially on the rich. What a horrible way to say thanks. "Thanks for my job you created and gave to me. Here's a tax hike." It's like a newborn baby smacking its mom in the face. "It's a boy!" Smack!

Now let me digress a bit to relate a story. I have a bumper sticker that says, "Freedom isn't free." One of my liberal friends saw it and asked, "If freedom isn't free, why do you hate taxes so much? Aren't taxes part of the price tag for freedom?" Long story short... I exercised my freedom to kick his ass. And I did it for free.

My bumper sticker – which I'd put on during the early days of the Iraq War -- wasn't about TAXES. It was about the lives of soldiers, the billions used from the magic money pot to fund the wars, and letting the government tap our phones, and arrest and torture anyone if the President found it necessary. That's what I meant by "not being free." TAXES were never part of the equation. It was more about a state of mind, not a state of my wallet.

End of digression.

However, one regular Republican... not a politician... just a guy like you and me came up with a solution to keep those in power from ever raising our taxes. That man is Grover Norquist, the most loveable, most cuddly, most furry Grover ever.

He came up with the Pledge. A pledge not to raise taxes. And Republicans, knowing they wouldn't raise taxes anyway... signed it! That takes courage!

Signing the Pledge became the hot thing to do in the '90s and 2000s. Like watching "Friends." And those Republicans couldn't break that pledge... EVER! They could break the occasional campaign promise, or marriage vows, or even bend some rules in the Constitution ("Maybe the 4th Amendment really refers to the epileptic kind of seizure"), but they could never never never never break the Grover Pledge. Given the choice between throwing his firstborn into a fiery pit of churning razor blades or breaking the Pledge, a Republican stood by the signature he put on a piece of paper that rests in a binder on Grover's shelf.

And the Pledge is required for any new Republican looking to run for office, or already in office. The Pledge has done so many good things, that I believe we should change the opening of the Pledge of Allegiance to:
"I pledge allegiance, to Grover Norquist..."

It's the least we can do.

CHAPTER 60
Obamacare = death to all

We have a healthcare crisis in this nation. But it's not the one liberals gripe about ("Wah... 18,000 Americans die every year due to lack of health insurance... healthcare costs are skyrocketing... I lost my coverage because my insurer said that pimple I had in high school is a pre-existing condition!"). The real crisis is that Obama wants to meddle with a system that's worked out just fine for the last 200 years!

Read my lips. We have the best healthcare system in the world. Why? Because our system is predicated on paying doctors really well, and paying the best doctors even more than that. Take away that incentive, and you're left with Canada.

It's why all the world leaders and foreign billionaires come to America for medical care. Because the best doctors are here. Because we imported them from India.

Of course there is a little trade-off here. In order to make the best medical care available to those who can afford it (scalpels costs money, people!), the effect can sometimes be that a handful of Americans (50 million) may go without health insurance.

But like I've said many times, when people choose to be poor, they have to face the consequences. You want food so bad, then sacrifice. Make a choice (medicine or food?). Or get a job. Or get a better job. Do I have to provide all the answers?

So while our system incentivizes (I learned that word in a marketing class I took once at the community college) people to be great doctors, we must understand they can't all be superstars. They can't all be the LeBron James of doctors. But this Race to the Top (hmm, I like that phrase... I may try to trademark it) creates a pool of great doctors, who all have one goal in mind: to get rich. And to make people better. Greed means they work harder in medical school so they can have the skill to practice on the wealthy patients who can afford to see them. But even the ones who fail to become superstar doctors like Dr. Oz and Dr. Phil and Dr. Drew still do a good job. In America, even our shitty doctors are pretty good.

But even the shitty doctors don't want to take in poor people. Where's the reward in that? And he's not going to get a warm fuzzy feeling inside by saving the life of someone who has to go on living as a poor person. However, Obama wants to make it that EVERYONE have access to adequate health care. Even poor people.

And the only way these spoiled brats want access to healthcare is with health insurance. Apparently the emergency room isn't good enough for them. But it should be. It's FREE! It's always open. And they can treat damn near anything, if it's broken or infected. However, I'll admit they lack a couple resources.

"Welcome to the Emergency Room."

"I'm dying of breast cancer. Can I have some treatment?"

"Just take a seat and someone will be with you... never."

But... if a gunshot gets you in the boob, the emergency room can help.

So the new health care law (Obamacare... what an egotistical jerk; he had the audacity to name the law after himself) mandates that insurance companies must provide coverage even if you have a pre-existing condition. That's right... they have to take everyone. And their premiums. What ever happened to business FREEDOM? Imagine if a restaurant had to take in any customer that came through their doors?

So businesses lose their freedom with Obamacare. And providing healthcare through a company's plan just got more expensive. Not because of ever-increasing healthcare and insurance costs. No, it's because of Obamacare! Nice job, Barry Hussein.

While businesses lose their freedom, the people have theirs... the freedom to get screwed! And not in a good way. They MUST buy health insurance. And if you can't afford it, the government says they'll help out. But if you don't buy it, you get fined or go to a death camp.

Are you not stunned? The government is forcing people to buy something that is good for them! Um, sorry, Mr. President, but I'm one of those people who don't get sick. I'm like Bruce Willis in "Unbreakable." I don't NEED insurance. And if I do get sick, I'll just tough it out. I don't need a doctor, or health insurance. Just a few spoonfuls of NyQuil, and I'm on my way. And that little plug for NyQuil better get me a few cases of the stuff in the mail.

I thought Obama knew a thing or two about the Constitution (he was a big ol' lawyer and he went to Harvard. Or so he says). Apparently he's not aware that the government can't make us DO ANYTHING.

Sure, economists agree that if we all have health insurance, the price of healthcare will go down for all of us, as well. So I guess we'll all just sacrifice our principals and just tear up the Constitution to save a few bucks and lives. It's a slippery slope, people (NOTE: saying something is a "slippery slope" works every time. Plus it makes one sound engaged in a political conversation. It's how a discussion of gay marriage can lead to one on necrophilia). Maybe the government will require we all learn to tap dance, or watch all the Helen Mirren movies, or require that businesses pay a wage that doesn't go below a certain minimum.

Besides, if I don't buy insurance, I know the risks. I could get sick, or in a car accident, or take one too many speedballs. And I promise that if any of that happens, I will pay for the medical care out of my own pocket. And if I can't afford it, I'll accept my fate. I won't beg for help. Though I would expect my neighbors to pitch in and take care of me. Otherwise they're all uncaring assholes.

Besides, I think making access to health care easier just makes us weaker. Back in the old days if you got sick and missed work, you didn't get paid. Eff that. I'm coming in and coughing and sneezing and diarrhea-ing my way through the day so I get my check. Because I won't let a little thing like a cold or the flu or lupus keep me from my duties.

But now all this access means more sick days. And thanks to the unions, people are getting them. Some companies in the U.S. offer 3, 4 even 10 sick days per year to their employees. That's bullshit. Sick days should max out at two per year. To be used only when you're so sick you can't even open your eyes, or get out of bed, or reattach your arm, or stop vomiting even for a minute. If you're "sick" enough to watch a Tuesday afternoon Real Housewives marathon, you're fine enough to come in to the office or factory or classroom or air traffic controller terminal.

Having too many sick days just makes people lazy. Their thresholds for being "sick" change. They'll take sick days when they're not really ill, when their fevers are only at 102 degrees. And that affects worker productivity, and that affects the economy, and suddenly we're in another Great Depression. Thanks to Obamacare.

If we want healthcare to get well soon, we need to pull the plug on Obamacare.

CHAPTER 61
Support the Troops.
By sending them to war.

I support the troops. I have about eight yellow ribbon magnets on the back of my car, which shows the world how much I support the troops. And if I see a soldier in fatigues in the airport, I always tell him, "Thank you for your service."

What I like best about war is it gives people like me a chance to talk about how much I support the troops, and it makes me feel superior to those who don't. To be clear, those who don't support our troops are the people opposed to war. You can't be for the troops and against the war. It's like being opposed to driving, but favoring transportation. It just doesn't make any sense.

So from my standpoint, war is a great thing. But weak-kneed presidents like Obama want to END WARS. Like the one in Iraq, where he got ALL OUR troops out at the end of 2011. What the hell is up with that? Now we're down to ONE WAR. The back of my car looks ridiculous with only one war going on right now. That's why I pray Iran pulls something (or we say they pulled something), so we can send in the troops while us patriots back home go back to showing our support. Oh, and if the wars make Iraq and Iran and Afghanistan a better place to live for their residents, as they experience a life that's no longer under the oppressive thumb of an evil regime, all the better.

Maybe if Obama listened to our soldiers, he'd send them to more wars. A friend of mine sent me a video that showed President George W. Bush speaking to troops, and they cheered him wildly. They LOVED that man, and it was because he had the bravery to send them to TWO wars, shorten their furloughs at home, cut funding for body armor, and reduce their benefits. Bush didn't spoil the soldiers. No kid gloves there. You trained, now dammit get out and fight! Huzzah for Bush!

That same video cut to clip of Obama talking to the troops. He was all serious (wearing a suit, he's so smug), and the troops didn't even clap for him. Well no wonder. He didn't send them off to war, where all the action is. In fact, Obama is trying to end wars. Imagine having to explain THAT to your grandkids. *"We had this great war going on, where we were bringing more and more freedom to a Middle East country every day. That country had been too scared to ask for our help, but we didn't let them down. At least we didn't until flower-power Obama brought the troops home. Imagine their shock and awe, having to assimilate to a culture they hadn't seen in years and failing to finish rebuilding the country that had been bombed to rubble."*

Back when we went to war with Iraq because of their WMDs and ties to Osama bin laden, Obama actually opposed the war. Lucky for us he wasn't a U.S. Senator then. He was just a community organizer, so his opinion didn't matter because all he was doing was setting up bowling leagues for his ACORN friends.

Like a lot of people, Obama opposed the Iraq war because there wasn't enough proof for him (I guess he's Horatio Cane all of a sudden) that Iraq had WMDs. Hello! Remember that yellowcake from Niger. And Saddam gassed his own people, like 15 years before. And we knew he had WMDs because the U.S. sold them to him back when we were friends. We had the invoices!

So we knew Saddam had WMDs. Now when we didn't find them after our invasion, liberals went all "I told you so" on conservatives. As if this proved WMDs were there. As if this proved we lied our way into war. As if.

Well, let me tell you another story from the Middle East, from about 2,000 years ago, about something else that wasn't there. Jesus! Jesus was crucified, died, and was buried. And three days later, his tomb was EMPTY! The empty tomb proved he had once been in there. Just like the missing WMDs proved they had been in Iraq. You can't have missing WMDs without having WMDs in the first place!

So what happened to the WMDs, the ones that could take out whole armies and cities and countries and worlds in less than 11 minutes? What happened to these weapons that had us so scared? (I meant to say "concerned", not "scared". Because real Americans don't get scared).

The answer is simple. Saddam had stupidly shipped them off to Syria before the war started. What a dumbass. You see, he knew we were going to attack. President Bush had given him a deadline and everything, practically letting Saddam know the minute the attack would start. And the second that deadline expired... BOOM! Shock & Awe, baby! Put out your blanket because the fireworks show is starting. So right before the bombs started to fall, Saddam shipped all those weapons to Syria. He assumed that us not finding the weapons (and the embarrassment that came with it) would do more damage to the United States than actually using them on us.

156

Boy, that was stupid on his part! If I had been him, I would have used the weapons my enemy accused me of having, the same weapons that were the motivation for the war itself, to cause death and destruction to the enemy soldiers. But instead, Saddam GETS RID OF his weapons right before the war started. DUMB! What a terrible strategy.

But the only way we would be embarrassed by this ploy would be if we let liberals make a big deal out of the missing weapons. And sure, they bitched and moaned. But after awhile we came to learn the Iraq war wasn't all about WMDs. It was about removing a dictator and granting the Iraqi people the freedom they were begging us to provide them. And oil perhaps, maybe, possibly if you want to be technical, might have played a small, tiny part.

I'm glad Bush didn't mention those reasons for going to war until long after the war started. Because I'm not so sure as many people would have supported the war ahead of time. Luckily, as we got used to the war, we kind of just decided, "Well, we're already there. Might as well find some other reasons to be there so we don't look stupid. Plus it'll be a real pain to bring all those troops and equipment back home... especially with Iran nestled right between Iraq and Afghanistan. If Bed Bath & Beyond is between Old Navy and Books a Million, you might as well stop, right?"

Of course, President Bush, in all his wisdom, didn't complicate the message ahead of time (like college-boy Obama). He knew he only needed one good reason to go to war, not a whole bunch. So he picked WMDs. Then, after the war had been going on a few years, he revealed those other reasons, too. The freedom. The Saddam-capturing. Getting the oil. Avenging his dad (what a great son. Talk about the ultimate Father's Day gift: "Dad, instead of a tie, I attacked Saddam.")

The liberals contend that Bush only brought up those other reasons once it became clear the WMDs wouldn't be found (hey, Syria's a big country... finding WMDs there isn't like finding your car keys in the couch). And they further contend that he wouldn't have had the backing of the country if the main reason to go to war had been Saddam's ouster or bringing democracy to Iraq. Talk about sour grapes! Their president executes some of the most savvy military leadership in our lifetimes, and all the liberals can do is complain. Of course Bush would have gotten support to go to war. Because he had a secret weapon. His awesomeness. And if that wasn't enough, he had Dick Cheney (I have a whole chapter devoted to Dick Cheney up next… it's the feel-good chapter of the whole book!). We all know that if Cheney wanted a war, he was going to get it. Because he is one powerful son of a bitch. Thank God for that.

So we got the Iraqis their freedom. (They still owe us, big time. I want my check!) And we helped them execute the crap out of Saddam and his boys. Take that, Hussein!

CHAPTER 62
Cheney, Dick

Liberals hate Dick Cheney. They go so far as to call him evil, if you can believe such vitriol. Maybe their word for evil is our word for "hero." But the more liberals hate someone, the more I like him. So I like Dick Cheney a lot.

First, he had the foresight to be CEO of a company (Halliburton) that provides food and equipment to the armed forces, long before we got into wars with Iraq and Afghanistan. See, he somehow knew that we would need such a company, and he made sure that Halliburton existed so that it could one day supply our troops (at a modest mark-up) and win the War on Terror.

Then he was smart enough to become George W Bush's vice president. Cheney actually headed up then–candidate Bush's vice-president search committee. And what did Cheney find? That no one was as qualified as he was. Good for him! Most people wouldn't have that kind of confidence… most people would have let some other guy take on the job instead, for fear of looking like some self-promoting, power-grabbing megalomaniac. Cheney did not have that fear.

Cheney was the perfect vice president at the perfect time. He knew all about war, since he was Secretary of Defense for the first Bush president. So if a war just happened to arrive on our doorstep, he would be ready.

And wouldn't you know it? September 11th happened. Finally, we had an excuse to invade Iraq, and finish the job we started there 10 years before. And wouldn't you *also* know it? Halliburton was best equipped to help in the war effort. They were so well-prepared that they didn't even have to bid against any other companies. They got to name their own price. Thank God for them.

See, whenever those atheist liberals go door-to-door trying to get people to not believe in God, I just point out that, "God gave us Dick Cheney when we needed him most." God knew what he was doing.

Meanwhile, the same liberals point out that Cheney reminds them of Mr. Burns from the Simpsons, or Darth Vader from Star Wars, or Mr. Potter from "It's a Wonderful Life." Like that's a bad thing. Mr. Burns is a billionaire, which is awesome. And Darth Vader was wicked cool... he could get people to die just by looking at them! Cheney almost had the same power. If he wanted an invasion, he got it. Who was going to stand in his way? W?

Even today, while George W. Bush keeps a low profile, Cheney is still out there making speeches all about the uselessness of Obama. And the meaner Cheney gets, the more I like it. Because one day soon, Cheney will pass on. And Obama will be in the awkward position of having to say something nice about him. And 50 teleprompters won't make that scene any less fake.

So my proposal, before it's too late, is to show Cheney our appreciation. Name an airport after him. Name a state. Name a car. Name a line of eyewear. Name our schools after him. Build a statue of him out of Mt. Rainier. Have kids in schools sing his praises. Give him Victoria's Secret models as his harem. Publicly execute John Kerry for what he said about his daughter back in the 2004 election. Have all people named

Dick or Richard change their names, to make Cheney the biggest Dick we have around here.

CHAPTER 63
Evolution is just a theory, like gravity

I go to church. And I took a few science classes growing up; the kind of science classes that showed you that most of the science is iffy at best. What I do remember is that there is a HUGE difference between fact and theory, much like there is a HUGE difference between fact and fiction. So we have facts, and on the other side we have "guesses", or "crazy stories" or "James Patterson novels."

For example, it is a fact that Obama is a big stupid poopy pants. At this point in the book, it should be abundantly clear (Lord knows I've said it enough times to be true). However, I could say that it is my "theory" that there is an alternate universe (like in "The Matrix") where Obama is *not* a big stupid poopy pants. That means that this guess of mine can't be disproven (though even with an infinite number of alternate universes, I'm sure Obama is a big stupid poopy pants in all of them).

But theories are a pretty flexible deal. Some theories sound good ("It is my theory that my wife will yell at me when I tell her to get off her ass and fetch me a beer."). Some can be called crazy ("It is my theory that babies have a greater brain capacity for learning than an adult.") But no matter how you frame it up, it's just easiest to assume that a "theory" is not true. It shouldn't even be taken that seriously, unless enough of your friends and Glenn Beck believe it.

Evolution is a theory. So that means it's not true. And countless scientists and Kirk Cameron have debunked the idea of evolution soundly. They all make obvious points:
• If we came from apes, why are there still apes? Why didn't they all change to people?
• Evolution isn't mentioned in the Bible.

• People don't even look like apes. Most of them don't, anyway.
• How could evolution, a process that took a billion years, have even happened on a planet that's been around for 6,000 years?
• If we evolved from apes, why is it that bananas fit perfectly in our hands (I'm not sure about this, but that's the takeaway I had from that one Kirk Cameron video).
• If we are an evolving species, why do sequels always seem to be worse than the originals?

I find it mind-boggling that liberals need all this *explained* to them. It's like talking to a three-year-old. A three-year-old who won't use common sense. They always have to complicate things. And my motto is: If it takes a long time to explain it, then it's probably wrong. Simple is the easiest way to go. So we can believe that man evolved over a period of billions of years from single-celled organisms to human beings made up of bone, muscle, skin, an intricate highway of blood vessels, and cerebral cortex that controls every move and thought we make, or we can believe that God made us and that's that.

And by the way, who cares? Whether we evolved or were made from God, what good does that do us now? Isn't it safer to believe God did it, so you get into Heaven? Hell, I'm starting to regret writing this chapter, because if a liberal suddenly stops believing in evolution, he may end up in Heaven with me. And it won't be Heaven with liberals up there. It's better just to condemn them to an eternity in Hell.

So all you liberals out there, keep believing in your evolution.

CHAPTER 64
The Dixie Chicks: Three mean-spirited bitches

How dare they? How dare they say they were ashamed to be from Texas because George W. Bush was born there? It's bad enough they killed off Sipowicz in that "Goodbye Earl" video, but this? This was treason. It should have been "Goodbye, Girls" as in death penalty. But NOOO. They didn't even get prison time. I guess if you're famous, you get all sorts of breaks. Who knew?

So the Dixie Chicks got off scot-free, with no consequence for what they did. What sort of example does this set for our children, the children who listen to the Dixie Chicks?

They were in a foreign country when they said it, too. The cowards. Because if they said it in God's Country, there would have been trouble. Not Sin Wagon trouble. Something a lot worse.

When I go to a concert, I don't want the performers talking too much. Just sing the song. You're a singer, not a talker. And just play the hits. Not something from the new album.

But there are exceptions. Because some singers really have something to say. Or they say something that really enhances the song. Like when Ted Nugent says he wants Obama to suck on his machine gun. That's a nice, appropriate lead-in for "Cat Scratch Fever."

Now Obama never once condemned the Dixie Chicks for what they did... the irreparable damage that was done to George W. Bush. I'm sure the former president won't admit it, but it had to hurt his feelings. And those of us who supported him (While he took some liberal views, like sending AIDS money to Africa... it didn't stop AIDS, did it?) I supported him too, and was among those defending him against the Chicks. I bought 100 copies of "Home" and burned them. I wrote them threatening letters. I stopped watching "Heroes".

Then after a year or so, I kind of forgot about it. Because there was plenty out there to piss me off, and the Dixie Chicks were suddenly pretty far down the list.

And then they came out with a new album. So the monster hadn't been killed. Like Phoenix rising from the ashes, they rose from the ashes. Like Phoenix. But that didn't alarm me. What did was the name of their first single from that new album. "Not Ready to Make Nice".

I was stunned. I guess these ladies can truly hold a grudge, can't they? Some people would let things go, but not them. They had to sing about how they weren't about to apologize. And it went farther than that. They didn't believe THEY had done anything wrong! The gall. I'm ashamed that they're from Texas. So HA! (I'm actually from Ohio, but don't we all have a little Texan in us?).

However, I think other musical acts learned a valuable lesson from the Dixie Chicks, because none of them had anything bad to say about George W. Bush or his vision of America. Because music isn't about protest, or politics, or telling a story. It's about finding the right hook. And left-wing radicalism does not have a beat anyone can dance to.

CHAPTER 65
"Happy Holidays" = WAR!

As I write this, it is a few days until Christmas. And I am nervous. I don't know if we'll have a Christmas this year. Because the liberal war on this holiday continues unabated. And while we've had a Christmas every year for 2000 years, this could be the year it doesn't happen.

The only news network that covers this War is Fox News. I guess war coverage isn't worth CNN's time. But please tell us more about the cat that whistles!

The first salvo in the war was fired by liberals. The first one of them to say, "Happy Holidays" instead of "Merry Christmas" fired the shot heard 'round the world.

Happy Holidays?

What the hell does that mean?

I asked one of my liberal friends and he said, "I say it because it encompasses the total holiday season, beginning with Thanksgiving, ending with New Year's Day, and including religious holidays like Christmas and Hanukah and Kwanzaa. It's a more inclusive greeting, and no one is left out. Plus it's nice."

Excuse me? Inclusive? Is that what our country is all about?

God said that "Jesus is the Reason for the Season." He means the holiday season! It's about Jesus! Those other "holidays" only exist because Jesus was born. Like when my neighbor bought a pool and we all showed up unannounced. Jesus and Christmas is that pool that attracts the other holidays, like the Death Star's tractor beam.

The power of Christmas is so strong that it pulled Thanksgiving and New Year's into its orbit. They got pulled into the Christmas season. They are a part of the Christmas season. And the rule states that the greeting must therefore be "Merry Christmas." The only exception is on the actual date of Thanksgiving or New Year's Day, when you can say "Happy Thanksgiving" and "Happy New Year" respectively.

Now liberals wonder, what's the big deal? The big deal is that "Happy Holidays" offends Baby Jesus. And that offends us conservative Christians. And if you think we'll shut up about it, you're way off.

And each year, Bill O'Reilly selflessly takes up our cause (and writes about it in his books, on sale now!). Sometimes we think, "Is he really going to talk about it again on The Factor?" And each year he's back, as his investigative reporters discover schools that can't re-enact a manger scene while reading from the Bible, or unearth a cashier at Target who says, "Happy Holidays." We caught you, Sophia from Nashville! What's it feel like to be a solider of evil?

Now liberals also contend that Jewish people don't necessarily like it when they're told "Merry Christmas". Well, I'm sorry if not all Jews look like Jews! If I had a better Jewdar I would say "Happy Hanukah!" But I don't. So accept my "Merry Christmas."

Now I'm not saying I'm not empathetic. I know where the Jews are coming from in this argument. So if a Jewish person said "Happy Hanukah" to me, I would politely say "thank you." And then I would smile and say, "I'm a true believer in Christ, unlike you who's waiting around for a savior that's not going to come, so unless we cross paths again on this planet sometime, we'll never see each other again because I'll be singing in heaven while you're burning in hell. Merry Christmas."

And Goodwill to Men.

CHAPTER 66
The solution? ME!

I'm not very fond of the Republican candidate we have right now. He's not good enough. So I'm willing to do what's best for this country. I'm running for president.

I'm also running for president because I'm pretty sure I'd like it when people clap for me. It would be awesome.

Have you seen those crowds on TV? They go nuts and hold signs and wear funny hats and buttons. Even for candidates that get about 6% of the primary vote. And they would all cheer for *me*.

I see it playing out like this: The crowd has been waiting for me. Some gathered early in the morning just to get a good seat. Then I would walk out to the podium, smile, act all aw-shucksy, as if to say, "All this for me? You shouldn't have." Just like Taylor Swift. I would let the cheers reach a fever pitch. I'd give a little smile to the pretty ladies. Wave to the children. Do a big ol' fist pump in the air.

Then I would subtly encourage the crowd to keep clapping while holding out my hands as if to say, "OK, that's enough, you're embarrassing me by clapping so much. I know I'm great; you've made that point loud and clear." Then I would start to talk and the cheering would start up again, interrupting me. But I would take it all in stride. Because I'm so cool. I can handle the adulation.

Then, just when the crowd has quieted down, I will say something to get them all riled up again, like "Are you ready to take this country back?" And then the cheers would be deafening. I would smile again, loving the praise, so happy that the people have found a savior (besides Jesus) who can make their hopes and dreams come true. Me.

I wouldn't go into a lot of facts and figures in my speech. Because that doesn't make a good speech. What truly counts is the number of times the crowd breaks into applause. In my speeches, I would try to make that happen 100 times. And I would make sure certain that cheerworthy buzzphrases are in the speech, like:

"Barack HUSSEIN Obama!"

"No taxes ever!"

"End the liberal agenda!"

"End the gay agenda!"

"End the endangered species agenda!"

"Drill!"

"Drill for oil!"

"Drill for anything!"

"Sarah Palin!"

"Simplify the tax code!"

"Class warfare!"

"You're the true Americans!"

"The troops!"

"State's rights!'

"No more big government!"

"I love this country!"

"Free candy!"

Plus I'm the only candidate that I agree with on 100% of the time. So if I want a candidate I like, I better have me to vote for.

I also like the idea of debating my enemies (I mean opponents). I'm a firm believer in putting people in their place and calling them out when their facts are wrong, or when they just piss me off. With Obama, there would be plenty of both. Man, to debate him would be the ultimate. I'd have a whole set of things to rebut him with:

"You can't handle the truth!"

"No, you, sir are out of order!"

"Are you better off than you were five years ago?"

"I know you are but what am I?"

"Obviously, my opponent prefers to wipe his ass with the Constitution. I prefer to use it to KICK SOME ASS!" (cue applause)

"Say Nope to Hope."

"That's what your mom said last night!"

"After I had sex with her."

"Piss off, guv'ner."

"The ocean called. They're running out of you!"

"Is that so, Barack HUSSEIN Obama?"

"STFU."

"Joe Biden has hair plugs."

"NOBAMA."

"Does Barry Manilow know you raid his wardrobe?"

"There you go again!"

"And again."

(Covering my ears) "I can't hear you!"

"Homo says what?" (real softly, under my breath)

"Suck my fat one."

"Would the candidate care to respond to the allegations that he's a big pile of turds?"

I would need a platform, but I think this book would be it. A lot of candidates write books for their campaigns. So I killed two birds with one stone these last few days (I also wrote this book). I doubt there's anything in here that a reporter can use against me in interviews and at debates. And if some reporter tries to get me with a "gotcha" question, I can just say, "It's in my book. You'll just have to buy it to get the answers you want. And make sure you buy the updated paperback edition, which will include a new introduction, and a bonus chapter. Plus get the children's edition, with illustrations."

On the campaign trail, I would totally rock. Sure I'd have a stump speech, where I lay out my ideas for making this country great again while taking her back. And the cheering would continue. I'd autograph some signs, kiss some babies, shake some hands. It's all about showing the electorate how accessible I am. I'm just like you, people. Except I'm on a private plane, I have my own bus, and when I'm president my decisions could ruin your lives in a heartbeat. But at our core, we're a lot alike.

Speaking of the buses and planes, let me just say, "Wow." First off, my bus would have an awesome paint job, and a lightning bolt or some flames on the side. Gotta make it look real badass. Don't mess with the bus, because my campaign is on FIRE! I'd have a waterbed in the back of the bus, to make it feel like I'm on a boat. And I'd have a couple big screen TVs. One for watching Fox News. And the other for my Playstation. The bus will be so wicked cool, I may not want to get off. But knowing that crowds are out there, waiting to cheer me on, is enough motivation to get me off that bus. That and the free food.

Free food is everywhere when you're a presidential candidate. In my life, I think I've seen about three diners. But when you're running for president, there are diners everywhere! And even if there are big crowds waiting for me in a diner, I get served first. No waiting. I wouldn't be one of those stuffy candidates either. I'd make sure my advisors tip 20% instead of the standard 15%, even if the service is a bit shoddy. I would sit at a table where a couple old guys wearing John Deere hats are sitting, and we'll talk about America. They'll be amazed at my wisdom, but will also be impressed by my charisma, and how a big important person like me can speak down to the level of his supporters. Hopefully they don't smell like cowshit.

The banter is what I will excel at. I am a great conversationalist. I can talk at length on a variety of topics. And if the conversation is on something I'm uninterested in, I'm also great at changing the subject.

Them: So what will you do to make sure financial practices like credit default swaps won't wreak havoc on our economy?
Me: Go Bears!

See what I did there? It's a common political practice. You may be asked a question you don't want to answer. So the trick is to slyly avoid answering that question by talking about something else. Politicians do it all the time. You have to be real subtle and shrewd, so no one really notices that hey, you didn't answer the question! By the time anyone realizes it, BOOM, we're onto the next part of the discussion.

So that practice will work on the campaign trail, and in interviews. Now I know some candidates catch a lot of flak for not doing enough interviews. Like Sarah Palin said she would only talk to Fox News. Me, I won't talk to anyone! I'll interview them! "Mr. Anderson [using my Matrix voice] Cooper, are we really to believe that someone as young as you has grey hair? It's an obvious ploy to make you look older and more distinguished. Admit it! You're a liar! LIAR!" That'll leave him speechless. And then maybe I'll make it on the illustrious "Riducu-List."

However, not everybody watches the newschannels. So to get my face and personality out there, I'd need to go on talk shows like Leno and Letterman and those other guys. I would read a Top Ten List on Lettermen, probably something appropriate and topical like, "Top Ten Reasons I'm so Awesome." And on Leno (Is it even called the "Tonight Show" anymore) I would banter with Mr. Big Chin himself, and ask if he's still doing those Doritos commercials. He'd laugh at all my stuff (while deep down hoping I win the election since I could easily take his place as host of "The Tonight Show", and that would scare him), and ask the questions people want the answers to like, "What is your favorite rock band." And I would say Damn Yankees, because they had American Hero Ted Nugent. So that would make me look hip and cool to the kids.

I may mess up a couple times on the campaign trail. I may mix up some country names, or mispronounce the name of a world leader ("I misspoke when I said the president of France was Ze French Guy"), or poop myself on national TV. Hell, it happens to everyone. But I know how my supporters can handle that momentary loss of faith in a candidate when it appears he or she is seriously unqualified for dog catcher, let alone president of the United States. My advice to them: *Just ignore it.*

If *my* favorite candidate embarrasses himself, I just don't watch it. I won't click on the link, or watch the news segment, or read about it. Out of sight, out of mind.

Because watching that stuff, it's just too painful. I always feel bad for the guy. So by not watching it, it never happened. So Rick Perry never forgot the Department of Energy. Herman Cain never struggled to figure out Obama's foreign policy in Libya. Michelle Bachmann never mixed up Lexington and Concord. And Newt Gingrich never had all those affairs or spent most of his campaign trying to sell books and DVDs. Mitt Romney never flip flopped. And Ron Paul... well, we know he just runs because he likes to run. He's the Republican Dennis Kucinich. Ron Paul is there to give the libertarians some hope their ideas will see the light of day. Plus it's good for the Ayn Rand estate when "Atlas Shrugged" sales go up.

So if I mess up by saying Iowa is in Africa, or I accidentally call my wife by my girlfriend's name, or drunkenly tell Brian Williams I want to kiss him, just let it go. Don't watch when it shows up on YouTube. Just wash it away. My mistakes don't define me. My carefully crafted, focus-group-tested image does. *I am what my campaign says I am.*

In fact, that will be one of my slogans. In fact, I wouldn't just settle on one. Obama had Hope and Change. And now that's bitten him in the ass. With me, I'll have a boatload of slogans... so many that none will define me or be remembered after the campaign is over. But they'll all be hard-hitting, and make the voters think. Slogans like:
• Trust him. With your lives.
• He makes a lot of decisions based on emotion.
• Why *not* me?
• Give him the chance to vote for himself for president
• Just wait'll you see what he does to the Supreme Court
• "If I were alive today, I would vote for him."
    -   Abraham Lincoln
• Kills liberals dead
• What's with all the gotcha questions?
• Can I see your papers?
• He hardly ever cheats on his wife.

- I'll never admit a mistake.
- Don't worry... he'll be safe if a nuclear war happens.
- He doesn't take losing very well.
- Make America Awesome Again

Now an important part of the campaign will be choosing my vice-president. It's a tricky business, because we want someone great and popular, but not as great and popular as me. If he was so great, then people might think HE should be president. So I better make sure he doesn't upstage me. My guidelines in a vice president are that he is:
- Older than me... too old to become president when my time is done
- Younger than me, but not as good looking
- Not funnier than I am
- Is on his first wife
- Chews with his mouth closed
- Comes from a state I need to win
- Is a little shorter than me
- Has all his hair
- Nods a lot when I talk

My choice. Tim Tebow.

On election night I will be very modest at winning every electoral vote. I'll call Obama and graciously avoid calling him a "big loser" for the first two minutes of our conversation.

And then I will be Inaugurated, and our long, national, poopy pants nightmare will be over.

Lawrence/Tebow '12. Don't forget to write it in.

13345773R00091

Made in the USA
Charleston, SC
03 July 2012